ON THE DUTIES OF THE CLERGY

by

St. Ambrose

Translated by:
The Rev. H. De Romestin
With the assistance of:
The Rev. E. De Romestin and
The Rev. H. T. F. Duckworth

This edition:

© 2010 Benediction Classics, Oxford.

Contents

PREFACE   i

BOOK ONE   1

BOOK TWO   83

BOOK THREE   130

PREFACE

St. Ambrose, esteeming very highly the dignity of the ministerial office, was most desirous that the clergy of his diocese should live worthily of their high vocation, and be good and profitable examples to the people. Consequently he undertook the following treatise, setting forth the duties of the clergy, and taking as a model the treatise of Cicero, *De Officiis*.

The writer says that his object is to impress upon those whom he has ordained the lessons which he had previously taught them. Like Cicero, he treats of that which is right, becoming, or honourable [*decorum*], and what is expedient [*utile*]; but with reference not to this life but to that which is to come, teaching in the first book that which is becoming or honourable; in the second, what is expedient; and in the third, considering both in conjunction.

In the first book he divides duties into ordinary, or the way of the commandments, binding upon all alike; and perfect, which consist in following the counsels. After treating then of some elementary duties, such as those towards parents and elders, he touches upon the two principles which lead the mind, reason and appetite, and shows that what is becoming consists in thinking of good and right things, and in the subjection of the appetite to reason, and supplies certain rules and examples, ending with a discussion on the four Cardinal Virtues, Prudence, Justice, Fortitude, and Temperance.

In the second book, passing from what is becoming to what is expedient, he points out that we can only measure what is really expedient by reference to eternal life, in contradiction to the errors of heathen philosophers, and shows that what is expedient consists in the knowledge of God and in good living. Incidentally he shows that what is becoming is really that which is expedient, and ends the book with several chapters of practical considerations.

In the third book he treats of duties of perfection, and lays down as a rule that in everything we must inquire what is expedient, not for individuals, but for many or for all. Nothing is to be striven after which is not becoming; to this everything must give place, not only expediency but even friendship and life itself. By many examples he then proves how holy men have sought after what was becoming, and have thereby secured what was expedient.

The object of St. Ambrose in basing his treatise on the lines of that of Cicero would seem to have been the confutation of some of the false principles of heathenism, and to show how much higher Christian morality is than that of the Gentiles. The treatise was probably composed about A.D. 391.

BOOK ONE

Chapter 1.

A Bishop's special office is to teach; St. Ambrose himself, however, has to learn in order that he may teach; or rather has to teach what he has not learned; at any rate learning and teaching with himself must go on together.

1. I think I shall not seem to be taking too much on myself, if, in the midst of my children, I yield to my desire to teach, seeing that the master of humility himself has said: Come, you children, hearken unto me: I will teach you the fear of the Lord. Wherein one may observe both the humility and the grace of his reverence for God. For in saying the fear of the Lord, which seems to be common to all, he has described the chief mark of reverence for God. As, however, fear itself is the beginning of wisdom and the source of blessedness— for they that fear the Lord are blessed — he has plainly marked himself out as the teacher for instruction in wisdom, and the guide to the attainment of blessedness.

2. We therefore, being anxious to imitate his reverence for God, and not without justification in dispensing grace, deliver to you as to children those things which the Spirit of Wisdom has imparted to him, and which have been made clear to us through him, and learned by sight and by example. For we can no longer now escape from the duty of teaching which the needs of the priesthood have laid upon us, though we tried to avoid it: For God gave some, apostles; and some, prophets; and some, evangelists; and some, pastors and teachers. (Ephesians 4:11)

3. I do not therefore claim for myself the glory of the apostles (for who can do this save those whom the Son of God Himself has chosen?); nor the grace of the prophets, nor the virtue of the evangelists, nor the cautious care of the pastors. I only desire to attain to that care and diligence in the sacred writings, which the Apostle has placed last among the duties of the saints; (1 Corinthians 12:10) and this very thing I desire, so that, in the endeavour to teach, I may be able to learn. For one is the true Master, Who alone has not learned, what He taught all; but men learn before they teach, and receive from Him what they may hand on to others.

4. But not even this was the case with me. For I was carried off from the judgment seat, and the garb [*infulis*] of office, to enter on the priesthood, and began to teach you, what I myself had not yet learned. So it happened that I began to teach before I began to learn. Therefore I must learn and teach at the same time, since I had no leisure to learn before.

Chapter 2.

Manifold dangers are incurred by speaking; the remedy for which Scripture shows to consist in silence.

5. Now what ought we to learn before everything else, but to be silent, that we may be able to speak? Lest my voice should condemn me, before that of another acquit me; for it is written: By your words you shall be condemned. (Matthew 12:37) What need is there, then, that you should hasten to undergo the danger of condemnation by speaking, when you can be more safe by keeping silent? How many have I seen to fall into sin by speaking, but scarcely one by keeping silent; and so it is more difficult to know how to keep silent than how to speak. I know that most persons speak because they do not know how to keep silent. It is seldom that any one is silent even when speaking profits him nothing. He is wise, then, who knows how to keep silent. Lastly, the Wisdom of God said: The Lord has given to me the tongue of learning, that I should know when it is good to speak. Justly, then, is he wise who has received of the Lord to know when he ought to speak. Wherefore the Scripture says well: A wise man will keep silence until there is opportunity. (Sirach 20:7)

6. Therefore the saints of the Lord loved to keep silence, because they knew that a man's voice is often the utterance of sin, and a man's speech is the beginning of human error. Lastly, the Saint of the Lord said: I said, I will take heed to my ways, that I offend not in my tongue. For he knew and had read that it was a mark of the divine protection for a man to be hid from the scourge of his own tongue, (Job 5:21) and the witness of his own conscience. We are chastised by the silent reproaches of our thoughts, and by the judgment of conscience. We are chastised also by the lash of our own voice, when we say things whereby our soul is mortally injured, and our mind is sorely wounded. But who is there that has his heart clean from the impurities of sin, and does not offend in his tongue? And so, as he saw there was no one who could keep his mouth free from evil speaking, he laid upon himself the law of innocency by a rule of silence, with a view to avoiding by silence that fault which he could with difficulty escape in speaking.

7. Let us hearken, then, to the master of precaution: I said, I will take heed to my ways; that is, I said to myself: in the silent biddings of my thoughts, I have enjoined upon myself, that I should take heed to my ways. Some ways there are which we ought to follow; others as to which we ought to take heed. We must follow the ways of the Lord, and take heed to our own ways, lest they lead us into sin. One can take heed if one is not hasty in speaking. The law says: Hear, O Israel, the Lord your God. (Deuteronomy 6:4) It said not: Speak, but Hear. Eve fell because she said to the man what she had not heard from the Lord her God. The first word from God says to you: Hear! If you hear, take heed to your ways; and if you have fallen, quickly amend your way. For: Wherein does a young man amend his way; except in taking heed to the word of the Lord? Be silent therefore first of all, and hearken, that you fail not in your tongue.

8. It is a great evil that a man should be condemned by his own mouth. Truly, if each one shall give account for an idle word, (Matthew 12:36) how much more for words of impurity and shame? For words uttered hastily are far worse than idle words. If, therefore, an account is demanded for an idle word, how much more will punishment be exacted for impious language?

Chapter 3.
Silence should not remain unbroken, nor should it arise from idleness. How heart and mouth must be guarded against inordinate affections.

9. What then? Ought we to be dumb? Certainly not. For: there is a time to keep silence and a time to speak. (Ecclesiastes 3:7) If, then, we are to give account for an idle word, let us take care that we do not have to give it also for an idle silence. For there is also an active silence, such as Susanna's was, who did more by keeping silence than if she had spoken. For in keeping silence before men she spoke to God, and found no greater proof of her chastity than silence. Her conscience spoke where no word was heard, and she sought no judgment for herself at the hands of men, for she had the witness of the Lord. She therefore desired to be acquitted by Him, Who she knew could not be deceived in any way. Yea, the Lord Himself in the Gospel worked out in silence the salvation of men. (Matthew 26:63) David rightly therefore enjoined on himself not constant silence, but watchfulness.

10. Let us then guard our hearts, let us guard our mouths. Both have been written about. In this place we are bidden to take heed to our mouth; in another place you are told: Keep your heart with all diligence. (Proverbs 4:23) If David took heed, will you not take heed? If Isaiah had unclean lips— who said: Woe is me, for I am undone, for I am a man, and have unclean lips (Isaiah 6:5) — if a prophet of the Lord had unclean lips, how shall we have them clean?

11. But for whom was it written, unless it was for each one of us: Hedge your possession about with thorns, and bind up your silver and gold, and make a door and a bar for your mouth, and a yoke and a balance for your words? (Sirach 28:24-25) Your possession is your mind, your gold your heart, your silver your speech: The words of the Lord are pure words, as silver tried in the fire. A good mind is also a good possession. And, further, a pure inner life is a valuable possession. Hedge in, then, this possession of yours, enclose it with thought, guard it with thorns, that is, with pious care, lest the fierce passions of the flesh should rush upon it and lead it captive, lest strong emotions should assault it, and, overstepping their bounds, carry off its vintage. Guard your inner self. Do not neglect or contemn it as though it were worthless, for it is a valuable possession; truly valuable indeed, for its fruit is not perishable and only for a time, but is lasting and of use for eternal

salvation. Cultivate, therefore, your possession, and let it be your tilling ground.

12. Bind up your words that they run not riot, and grow wanton, and gather up sins for themselves in too much talking. Let them be rather confined, and held back within their own banks. An overflowing river quickly gathers mud. Bind up also your meaning; let it not be left slack and unchecked, lest it be said of you: There is no healing balsam, nor oil, nor bandage to apply. Sobriety of mind has its reins, whereby it is directed and guided.

13. Let there be a door to your mouth, that it may be shut when need arises, and let it be carefully barred, that none may rouse your voice to anger, and thou pay back abuse with abuse. You have heard it read today: Be angry and sin not. Therefore although we are angry (this arising from the motions of our nature, not of our will), let us not utter with our mouth one evil word, lest we fall into sin; but let there be a yoke and a balance to your words, that is, humility and moderation, that your tongue may be subject to your mind. Let it be held in check with a tight rein; let it have its own means of restraint, whereby it can be recalled to moderation; let it utter words tried by the scales of justice, that there may be seriousness in our meaning, weight in our speech, and due measure in our words.

Chapter 4.

The same care must be taken that our speech proceed not from evil passions, but from good motives; for here it is that the devil is especially on the watch to catch us.

14. If any one takes heed to this, he will be mild, gentle, modest. For in guarding his mouth, and restraining his tongue, and in not speaking before examining, pondering, and weighing his words— as to whether this should be said, that should be answered, or whether it be a suitable time for this remark— he certainly is practising modesty, gentleness, patience. So he will not burst out into speech through displeasure or anger, nor give sign of any passion in his words, nor proclaim that the flames of lust are burning in his language, or that the incentives of wrath are present in what he says. Let him act thus for fear that his words, which ought to grace his inner life, should at the last plainly show and prove that there is some vice in his morals.

15. For then especially does the enemy lay his plans, when he sees passions engendered in us; then he supplies tinder; then he lays snares. Wherefore the prophet says not without cause, as we heard read today: Surely He has delivered me from the snare of the hunter and from the hard word. Symmachus said this means the word of provocation; others the word that brings disquiet. The snare of the enemy is our speech— but that itself is also just as much an enemy to us. Too often we say something that our foe takes hold of, and whereby he wounds us as though by our own sword. How far better it is to perish by the sword of others than by our own!

16. Accordingly the enemy tests our arms and clashes together his weapons. If he sees that I am disturbed, he implants the points of his darts, so as to raise a crop of quarrels. If I utter an unseemly word, he sets his snare. Then he puts before me the opportunity for revenge as a bait, so that in desiring to be revenged, I may put myself in the snare, and draw the death-knot tight for myself. If any one feels this enemy is near, he ought to give greater heed to his mouth, lest he make room for the enemy; but not many see him.

Chapter 5.

We must guard also against a visible enemy when he incites us by silence; by the help of which alone we can escape from those greater than ourselves, and maintain that humility which we must display towards all.

17. But we must also guard against him who can be seen, and who provokes us, and spurs us on, and exasperates us, and supplies what will excite us to licentiousness or lust. If, then, any one reviles us, irritates, stirs us up to violence, tries to make us quarrel; let us keep silence, let us not be ashamed to become dumb. For he who irritates us and does us an injury is committing sin, and wishes us to become like himself.

18. Certainly if you are silent, and hidest your feelings, he is wont to say: Why are you silent? Speak if you dare; but you dare not, you are dumb, I have made you speechless. If you are silent, he is the more excited. He thinks himself beaten, laughed at, little thought of, and ridiculed. If you answer, he thinks he has become the victor, because he has found one like himself. For if you are silent, men will say: That

man has been abusive, but this one held him in contempt. If you return the abuse, they will say: Both have been abusive. Both will be condemned, neither will be acquitted. Therefore it is his object to irritate, so that I may speak and act as he does. But it is the duty of a just man to hide his feelings and say nothing, to preserve the fruit of a good conscience, to trust himself rather to the judgment of good men than to the insolence of a calumniator, and to be satisfied with the stability of his own character. For that is: To keep silence even from good words; since one who has a good conscience ought not to be troubled by false words, nor ought he to make more of another's abuse than of the witness of his own heart.

19. So, then, let a man guard also his humility. If, however, he is unwilling to appear too humble, he thinks as follows, and says within himself: Am I to allow this man to despise me, and say such things to my face against me, as though I could not open my mouth before him? Why should I not also say something whereby I can grieve him? Am I to let him do me wrong, as though I were not a man, and as though I could not avenge myself? Is he to bring charges against me as though I could not bring together worse ones against him?

20. Whoever speaks like this is not gentle and humble, nor is he without temptation. The tempter stirs him up, and himself puts such thoughts in his heart. Often and often, too, the evil spirit employs another person, and gets him to say such things to him; but do thou set your foot firm on the rock. Although a slave should abuse, let the just man be silent, and if a weak man utter insults, let him be silent, and if a poor man should make accusations, let him not answer. These are the weapons of the just man, so that he may conquer by giving way, as those skilled in throwing the javelin are wont to conquer by giving way, and in flight to wound their pursuers with severer blows.

Chapter 6.
In this matter we must imitate David's silence and humility, so as not even to seem deserving of harm.

21. What need is there to be troubled when we hear abuse? Why do we not imitate him who says: I was dumb and humbled myself, and kept silence even from good words? Or did David only say this, and not act up to it? No, he also acted up to it. For when Shimei the son of Gera

reviled him, David was silent; and although he was surrounded with armed men he did not return the abuse, nor sought revenge: nay, even when the son of Zeruiah spoke to him, because he wished to take vengeance on him, David did not permit it. He went on as though dumb, and humbled; he went on in silence; nor was he disturbed, although called a bloody man, for he was conscious of his own gentleness. He therefore was not disturbed by insults, for he had full knowledge of his own good works.

22. He, then, who is quickly roused by wrong makes himself seem deserving of insult, even while he wishes to be shown not to deserve it. He who despises wrongs is better off than he who grieves over them. For he who despises them looks down on them, as though he feels them not; but he who grieves over them is tormented, just as though he actually felt them.

Chapter 7.

How admirably Psalm xxxix. [xxxviii.] takes the place of an introduction. Incited thereto by this psalm the saint determines to write on duties. He does this with more reason even than Cicero, who wrote on this subject to his son. How, further, this is so.

23. Not without thought did I make use of the beginning of this psalm, in writing to you, my children. For this psalm which the Prophet David gave to Jeduthun to sing, I urge you to regard, being delighted myself with its depth of meaning and the excellency of its maxims. For we have learned in those words we have just shortly touched upon, that both patience in keeping silence and the duty of awaiting a fit time for speaking are taught in this psalm, as well as contempt of riches in the following verses, which things are the chief groundwork of virtues. Whilst, therefore, meditating on this psalm, it has come to my mind to write on the Duties.

24. Although some philosophers have written on this subject— Panætius, for instance, and his son among the Greek, Cicero among the Latin, writers— I did not think it foreign to my office to write also myself. And as Cicero wrote for the instruction of his son, so I, too, write to teach you, my children. For I love you, whom I have begotten in the Gospel, no less than if you were my own true sons. For nature does not make us love more ardently than grace. We certainly ought to

love those who we think will be with us for evermore than those who will be with us in this world only. These often are born unworthy of their race, so as to bring disgrace on their father; but you we chose beforehand, to love. They are loved naturally, of necessity, which is not a sufficiently suitable and constant teacher to implant a lasting love. But you are loved on the ground of our deliberate choice, whereby a great feeling of affection is combined with the strength of our love: thus one tests what one loves and loves what one has chosen.

Chapter 8.

The word Duty has been often used both by philosophers and in the holy Scriptures; from whence it is derived.

25. Since, therefore, the person concerned is one fit to write on the Duties, let us see whether the subject itself stands on the same ground, and whether this word is suitable only to the schools of the philosophers, or is also to be found in the sacred Scriptures. Beautifully has the Holy Spirit, as it happens, brought before us a passage in reading the Gospel today, as though He would urge us to write; whereby we are confirmed in our view, that the word *officium*, duty, may also be used with us. For when Zacharias the priest was struck dumb in the temple, and could not speak, it is said: And it came to pass that as soon as the days of his duty [*officii*] were accomplished, he departed to his own house. We read, therefore, that the word *officium*, duty, can be used by us.

26. And this is not inconsistent with reason, since we consider that the word *officium* (duty) is derived from *efficere* (to effect), and is formed with the change of one letter for the sake of euphony; or at any rate that you should do those things which injure [*officiant*] no one, but benefit all.

Chapter 9.

A duty is to be chosen from what is virtuous, and from what is useful, and also from the comparison of the two, one with the other; but nothing is recognized by Christians as virtuous or useful which is not helpful to the future life. This treatise on duty, therefore, will not be superfluous.

27. The philosophers considered that duties were derived from what is virtuous and what is useful, and that from these two one should choose the better. Then, they say, it may happen that two virtuous or two useful things will clash together, and the question is, which is the more virtuous, and which the more useful? First, therefore, duty is divided into three sections: what is virtuous, what is useful, and what is the better of two. Then, again, these three are divided into five classes; that is, two that are virtuous, two that are useful, and, lastly, the right judgment as to the choice between them. The first they say has to do with the moral dignity and integrity of life; the second with the conveniences of life, with wealth, resources, opportunities; while a right judgment must underlie the choice of any of them. This is what the philosophers say.

28. But we measure nothing at all but that which is fitting and virtuous, and that by the rule of things future rather than of things present; and we state nothing to be useful but what will help us to the blessing of eternal life; certainly not that which will help us enjoy merely the present time. Nor do we recognize any advantages in opportunities and in the wealth of earthly goods, but consider them as disadvantages if not put aside, and to be looked on as a burden, when we have them, rather than as a loss when expended.

29. This work of ours, therefore, is not superfluous, seeing that we and they regard duty in quite different ways. They reckon the advantages of this life among the good things, we reckon them among the evil things; for he who receives good things here, as the rich man in the parable, is tormented there; and Lazarus, who endured evil things here, there found comfort. (Luke 16:25) Lastly, those who do not read their writings may read ours if they will— if, that is, they do not require great adornment of language or a skilfully-treated subject, but are satisfied with the simple charm of the subject itself.

Chapter 10.

What is seemly is often found in the sacred writings long before it appears in the books of the philosophers. Pythagoras borrowed the law of his silence from David. David's rule, however, is the best, for our first duty is to have due measure in speaking.

30. We are instructed and taught that what is seemly is put in our Scriptures in the first place. (In Greek it is called πρέπον.) For we read: A Hymn beseems You, O God, in Sion. In Greek this is: Σοί πρέπει ὕμνος ὁ θεὸς ἐν Σιών. And the Apostle says: Speak the things which become sound doctrine. (Titus 2:1) And elsewhere: For it beseemed Him through Whom are all things and for Whom are all things, in bringing many sons unto glory, to make the Captain of their salvation perfect through sufferings. (Hebrews 2:10)

31. Was Panætius or Aristotle, who also wrote on duty, earlier than David? Why, Pythagoras himself, who lived before the time of Socrates, followed the prophet David's steps and gave his disciples a law of silence. He went so far as to restrain his disciples from the use of speech for five years. David, on the other hand, gave his law, not with a view to impair the gift of nature, but to teach us to take heed to the words we utter. Pythagoras again made his rule, that he might teach men to speak by not speaking. But David made his, so that by speaking we might learn the more how to speak. How can there be instruction without exercise, or advance without practice?

32. A man wishing to undergo a warlike training daily exercises himself with his weapons. As though ready for action he rehearses his part in the fight and stands forth just as if the enemy were in position before him. Or, with a view to acquiring skill and strength in throwing the javelin, he either puts his own arms to the proof, or avoids the blows of his foes, and escapes them by his watchful attention. The man that desires to navigate a ship on the sea, or to row, tries first on a river. They who wish to acquire an agreeable style of singing and a beautiful voice begin by bringing out their voice gradually by singing. And they who seek to win the crown of victory by strength of body and in a regular wrestling match, harden their limbs by daily practice in the wrestling school, foster their endurance, and accustom themselves to hard work.

33. Nature herself teaches us this in the case of infants. For they first exercise themselves in the sounds of speech and so learn to speak. Thus these sounds of speech are a kind of practice, and a school for the voice. Let those then who want to learn to take heed in speaking not refuse what is according to nature, but let them use all watchful care; just as those who are on a watchtower keep on the alert by watching, and not by going to sleep. For everything is made more perfect and strong by exercises proper and suitable to itself.

34. David, therefore, was not always silent, but only for a time; not perpetually nor to all did he refuse to speak; but he used not to answer the enemy that provoked him, the sinner that exasperated him. As he says elsewhere: As though he were deaf he heard not them that speak vanity and imagine deceit: and as though he were dumb he opened not his mouth to them. Again, in another place, it is said: Answer not a fool according to his folly, lest you also be like to him. (Proverbs 26:4)

35. The first duty then is to have due measure in our speech. In this way a sacrifice of praise is offered up to God; thus a godly fear is shown when the sacred Scriptures are read; thus parents are honoured. I know well that many speak because they know not how to keep silence. But it is not often any one is silent when speaking does not profit him. A wise man, intending to speak, first carefully considers what he is to say, and to whom he is to say it; also where and at what time. There is therefore such a thing as due measure in keeping silence and also in speaking; there is also such a thing as a due measure in what we do. It is a glorious thing to maintain the right standard of duty.

Chapter 11.

It is proved by the witness of Scripture that all duty is either ordinary or perfect. To which is added a word in praise of mercy, and an exhortation to practise it.

36. Every duty is either ordinary or perfect, a fact which we can also confirm by the authority of the Scriptures. For we read in the Gospel that the Lord said: If you will enter into life, keep the commandments. He says: Which? Jesus said to him: You shall do no murder, You shall not commit adultery, You shall not steal, You shall not bear false witness, Honour your father and your mother, You shall love your

neighbour as yourself. These are ordinary duties, to which something is wanting.

37. Upon this the young man says to Him: All these things have I kept from my youth up, what lack I yet? Jesus said unto him: If you will be perfect, go and sell all your goods and give to the poor, and you shall have treasure in heaven; and come and follow Me. (Matthew 19:20-21) And earlier the same is written, where the Lord says that we must love our enemies, and pray for those that falsely accuse and persecute us, and bless those that curse us. (Matthew 5:44) This we are bound to do, if we would be perfect as our Father Who is in heaven; Who bids the sun to shed his rays over the evil and the good, and makes the lands of the whole universe fertile with rain and dew without any distinction. (Matthew 5:45) This, then, is a perfect duty (the Greeks call it κατόρθωμα), whereby all things are put right which could have any failings in them.

38. Mercy, also, is a good thing, for it makes men perfect, in that it imitates the perfect Father. Nothing graces the Christian soul so much as mercy; mercy as shown chiefly towards the poor, that you may treat them as sharers in common with you in the produce of nature, which brings forth the fruits of the earth for use to all. Thus you may freely give to a poor man what you have, and in this way help him who is your brother and companion. Thou bestowest silver; he receives life. You give money; he considers it his fortune. Your coin makes up all his property.

39. Further, he bestows more on you than thou on him, since he is your debtor in regard to your salvation. If you clothe the naked, you clothe yourself with righteousness; if you bring the stranger under your roof, if you support the needy, he procures for you the friendship of the saints and eternal habitations. That is no small recompense. You sow earthly things and receive heavenly. Do you wonder at the judgment of God in the case of holy Job? Wonder rather at his virtue, in that he could say: I was an eye to the blind, and a foot to the lame. I was a father to the poor. Their shoulders were made warm with the skins of my lambs. The stranger dwelt not at my gates, but my door was open to every one that came. (Job 29:15-16) Clearly blessed is he from whose house a poor man has never gone with empty hand. Nor again is any one more blessed than he who is sensible of the needs of the poor, and the hardships of the weak and helpless. In the day of judgment he will

receive salvation from the Lord, Whom he will have as his debtor for the mercy he has shown.

Chapter 12.

To prevent any one from being checked in the exercise of mercy, he shows that God cares for human actions; and proves on the evidence of Job that all wicked men are unhappy in the very abundance of their wealth.

40. But many are kept back from the duty of showing active mercy, because they suppose that God does not care about the actions of men, or that He does not know what we do in secret, and what our conscience has in view. Some again think that His judgment in no wise seems to be just; for they see that sinners have abundance of riches, that they enjoy honours, health, and children; while, on the other hand, the just live in poverty and unhonoured, they are without children, sickly in body, and often in grief.

41. That is no small point. For those three royal friends of Job declared him to be a sinner, because they saw that he, after being rich, became poor; that after having many children, he had lost them all, and that he was now covered with sores and was full of weals, and was a mass of wounds from head to foot. But holy Job made this declaration to them: If I suffer thus because of my sins, why do the wicked live? They grow old also in riches, their seed is according to their pleasure, their children are before their eyes, their houses are prosperous; but they have no fear; there is no scourge from the Lord on them. (Job 21:7-9)

42. A faint-hearted man, seeing this, is disturbed in mind, and turns his attention away from it. Holy Job, when about to speak in the words of such a one, began thus, saying: Bear with me, I also will speak; then laugh at me. For if I am found fault with, I am found fault with as a man. Bear, therefore, the burden of my words. For I am going to say (he means) what I do not approve; but I shall utter wrong words to refute you. Or, to translate it in another way: How now? Am I found fault with by a man? That is: a man cannot find fault with me because I have sinned, although I deserve to be found fault with; for you do not find fault with me on the ground of an open sin, but estimate what I deserve for my offenses by the extent of my misfortunes. Thus the faint-hearted man, seeing that the wicked succeed and prosper, while

he himself is crushed by misfortune, says to the Lord: Depart from me, I desire not the knowledge of Your ways. (Job 21:14) What good is it that we serve Him, or what use to hasten to Him? In the hands of the wicked are all good things, but He sees not their works.

43. Plato has been greatly praised, because in his book on the State, he has made the person who undertook the part of objector against justice to ask pardon for his words, of which he himself did not approve; and to say that that character was only assumed for the sake of finding out the truth and to investigate the question at issue. And Cicero so far approved of this, that he also, in his book which he wrote on the Commonwealth, thought something must be said against that idea.

44. How many years before these did Job live! He was the first to discover this, and to consider what excuses had to be made for this, not for the sake of decking out his eloquence, but for the sake of finding out the truth. At once he made the matter plain, stating that the lamp of the wicked is put out, that their destruction will come; (Job 21:17) that God, the teacher of wisdom and instruction, is not deceived, but is a judge of the truth. Therefore the blessedness of individuals must not be estimated at the value of their known wealth, but according to the voice of their conscience within them. For this, as a true and uncorrupted judge of punishments and rewards, decides between the deserts of the innocent and the guilty. The innocent man dies in the strength of his own simplicity, in the full possession of his own will; having a soul filled as it were with marrow. (Job 21:24) But the sinner, though he has abundance in life, and lives in the midst of luxury, and is redolent with sweet scents, ends his life in the bitterness of his soul, and brings his last day to a close, taking with him none of those good things which he once enjoyed— carrying away nothing with him but the price of his own wickedness.

45. In thinking of this, deny if you can that a recompense is paid by divine judgment. The former feels happy in his heart, the latter wretched; that man on his own verdict is guiltless, this one a criminal; that man again is happy in leaving the world, this man grieves over it. Who can be pronounced guiltless that is not innocent in the sight of his own conscience? Tell me, he says, where is the covering of his tabernacle; his token will not be found. (Job 21:28) The life of the criminal is as a dream. He has opened his eyes. His repose has departed, his enjoyment has fled. Nay, that very repose of the wicked, which even

while they live is only seeming, is now in hell, for alive they go down into hell.

46. You see the enjoyments of the sinner; but question his conscience. Will he not be more foul than any sepulchre? You behold his joy, you admire the bodily health of his children, and the amount of his wealth; but look within at the sores and wounds of his soul, the sadness of his heart. And what shall I say of his wealth, when you read, For a man's life consists not in the abundance of the things which he possesses? (Luke 12:15) When you know, that though he seems to you to be rich, to himself he is poor, and in his own person refutes your judgment? What also shall I say of the number of his children and of his freedom from pain— when he is full of grief and decides that he will have no heir, and does not wish that those who copy his ways should succeed him? For the sinner really leaves no heir. Thus the wicked man is a punishment to himself, but the upright man is a grace to himself— and to either, whether good or bad, the reward of his deeds is paid in his own person.

Chapter 13.

The ideas of those philosophers are refuted who deny to God the care of the whole world, or of any of its parts.

47. But let us return to our point, lest we seem to have lost sight of the break we made in answering the ideas of those who, seeing some wicked men, rich, joyous, full of honours, and powerful, while many upright men are in want and are weak—suppose therefore that God either cares nothing about us (which is what the Epicureans say), or that He is ignorant of men's actions as the wicked say— or that, if He knows all things, He is an unjust judge in allowing the good to be in want and the wicked to have abundance. But it did not seem out of place to make a digression to meet an idea of this kind and to contrast it with the feelings of those very persons whom they consider happy— for they think themselves wretched. I suppose they would believe themselves more readily than us.

48. After this digression I consider it an easy matter to refute the rest— above all the declaration of those who think that God has no care whatever for the world. For instance, Aristotle declares that His providence extends only to the moon. But what workman is there who

gives no care to his work? Who would forsake and abandon what he believes himself to have produced? If it is derogatory to rule, is it not more so to have created? Though there is no wrong involved in not creating anything, it is surely the height of cruelty not to care for what one has created.

49. But if some deny God to be the Creator, and so count themselves among the beasts and irrational creatures, what shall we say of those who condemn themselves to such indignity? They themselves declare that God pervades all things, that all depend upon His power, that His might and majesty penetrate all the elements—lands, heaven, and seas; yet they think it derogatory to Him to enter into man's spirit, which is the noblest thing He has given us, and to be there with the full knowledge of the divine Majesty.

50. But philosophers who are held to be reasonable laugh at the teacher of these ideas as besotted and licentious. But what shall I say of Aristotle's idea? He thinks that God is satisfied with His own narrow bounds, and lives within the prescribed limits of His kingdom. This, however, is also what the poets' tales tell us. For they relate that the world is divided between three gods, so that it has fallen to the lot of one to restrain and rule heaven, to another the sea, and to a third the lower regions. They have also to take care not to stir up war one with the other by allowing thoughts and cares about the belongings of others to take hold of them. In the same way, Aristotle also declares that God has no care for the earth, as He has none for the sea or the lower regions. How is it that these philosophers shut out of their ranks the poets whose footsteps they follow?

Chapter 14.

Nothing escapes God's knowledge. This is proved by the witness of the Scriptures and the analogy of the sun, which, although created, yet by its light or heat enters into all things.

51. Next comes the answer to the question, whether God, not having failed to show care for His work, now fails to have knowledge of it? Thus it is written: He that planted the ear, shall He not hear? He that made the eye, shall He not regard?

52. This false idea was not unknown to the holy prophets. David himself introduces men to speak whom pride has filled and claimed for its own. For what shows greater pride than when men who are living in sin think it unfit that other sinners should live, and say: Lord, how long shall the ungodly, how long shall the ungodly triumph? And later on: And yet they say, the Lord shall not see: neither shall the God of Jacob regard it. Whom the prophet answers, saying: Take heed, you unwise among the people: O you fools, when will you understand? He that planted the ear, shall He not hear? Or He that made the eye, shall He not see? He that rebukes the nations, shall He not punish?— He that teaches man knowledge? The Lord knows the thoughts of man that they are vain. Does He Who discerns whatsoever is vain not know what is holy, and is He ignorant of what He Himself has made? Can the workman be ignorant of his own work? This one is a man, yet he discerns what is hidden in his work; and God— shall He not know His own work? Is there more depth, then, in the work than in its author? Has He made something superior to Himself; the value of which, as its Author, He was ignorant of, and whose condition He knew not, though He was its Director? So much for these persons.

53. But we are satisfied with the witness of Him Who says: I search out the heart and the reins. (Jeremiah 17:10) In the Gospel, also, the Lord Jesus says: Why do you think evil in your hearts? For He knew they were thinking evil. (Matthew 9:4) The evangelist also witnesses to this, saying: For Jesus knew their thoughts. (Luke 6:8)

54. The idea of these people will not trouble us much if we look at their actions. They will not have Him to be judge over them, Whom nothing deceives; they will not grant to Him the knowledge of things hidden, for they are afraid their own hidden things may be brought to light. But the Lord, also, knowing their works, has given them over unto darkness. In the night, he says, he will be as a thief, and the eye of the adulterer will watch for the darkness, saying, No eye shall see me; he has covered up his face. (Job 24:14-15) For every one that avoids the light loves darkness, seeking to be hid, though he cannot be hid from God, Who knows not only what is transacted, but also what will be thought of, both in the depths of space and in the minds of men. Thus, again, he who speaks in the book Ecclesiasticus says: Who sees me? The darkness has covered me, and the walls have hidden me; whom do I fear? (Sirach 23:18) But although lying on his bed he may think thus, he is caught where he never thought of it. It shall be, it

says, a shame to him because he knew not what the fear of the Lord was. (Sirach 23:31)

55. But what can be more foolish than to suppose that anything escapes God's notice, when the sun which supplies the light enters even hidden spots, and the strength of its heat reaches to the foundations of a house and its inner chambers? Who can deny that the depths of the earth, which the winter's ice has bound together, are warmed by the mildness of spring? Surely the very heart of a tree feels the force of heat or cold, to such an extent that its roots are either nipped with the cold or sprout forth in the warmth of the sun. In short, wherever the mildness of heaven smiles on the earth, there the earth produces in abundance fruits of different kinds.

56. If, then, the sun's rays pour their light over all the earth and enter into its hidden spots; if they cannot be checked by iron bars or the barrier of heavy doors from getting within, how can it be impossible for the Glory of God, which is instinct with life, to enter into the thoughts and hearts of men that He Himself has created? And how shall it not see what He Himself has created? Did He make His works to be better and more powerful than He Himself is, Who made them (in this event) so as to escape the notice of their Creator whenever they will? Did He implant such perfection and power in our mind that He Himself could not comprehend it when He wished?

Chapter 15.

Those who are dissatisfied with the fact that the good receive evil, and the evil good, are shown by the example of Lazarus, and on the authority of Paul, that punishments and rewards are reserved for a future life.

57. We have fully discussed two questions; and this discussion, as we think, has not turned out quite unfavourably for us. A third question yet remains; it is this: Why do sinners have abundance of wealth and riches, and fare sumptuously, and have no grief or sorrow; while the upright are in want, and are punished by the loss of wives or children? Now, that parable in the Gospel ought to satisfy persons like these; for the rich man was clothed in purple and fine linen, and dined sumptuously every day; but the beggar, full of sores, used to gather the crumbs of his table. After the death of the two, however, the beggar

was in Abraham's bosom in rest; the rich man was in torment. Is it not plain from this that rewards and punishments according to deserts await one after death?

58. And surely this is but right. For in a contest there is much labour needed— and after the contest victory falls to some, to others disgrace. Is the palm ever given or the crown granted before the course is finished? Paul writes well; He says: I have fought a good fight, I have finished my course, I have kept the faith; henceforth there is laid up for me a crown of righteousness, which the Lord, the righteous judge, shall give me at that day; and not to me only, but unto all them also that love His appearing. (2 Timothy 4:7-8) In that day, he says, He will give it— not here. Here he fought, in labours, in dangers, in shipwrecks, like a good wrestler; for he knew how that through much tribulation we must enter into the kingdom of God. (Acts 14:22) Therefore no one can receive a reward, unless he has striven lawfully; nor is the victory a glorious one, unless the contest also has been toilsome.

Chapter 16.

To confirm what has been said above about rewards and punishments, he adds that it is not strange if there is no reward reserved for some in the future; for they do not labour here nor struggle. He goes on to say also that for this reason temporal goods are granted to these persons, so that they may have no excuse whatever.

59. Is not he unjust who gives the reward before the end of the contest? Therefore the Lord says in the Gospel: Blessed are the poor in spirit, for theirs is the kingdom of heaven. (Matthew 5:3) He said not: Blessed are the rich, but the poor. By the divine judgment blessedness begins there whence human misery is supposed to spring. Blessed are they that hunger, for they shall be filled; Blessed are they that mourn, for they shall be comforted; Blessed are the merciful, for God will have mercy on them; Blessed are the pure in heart, for they shall see God; Blessed are they that are persecuted for righteousness' sake, for theirs is the kingdom of heaven; Blessed are you when men shall revile you, and persecute you, and shall say all manner of evil against you for righteousness' sake. Rejoice and be exceeding glad, for plentiful is your reward in heaven. A reward future and not present—in heaven, not on earth—has He promised shall be given. What further do you expect? What further is due? Why do you demand the crown

Book One

with so much haste, before thou dost conquer? Why do you desire to shake off the dust and to rest? Why do you long to sit at the feast before the course is finished? As yet the people are looking on, the athletes are in the arena, and thou— do you already look for ease?

60. Perhaps you say, Why are the wicked joyous? Why do they live in luxury? Why do they not toil with me? It is because they who have not put down their names to strive for the crown are not bound to undergo the labours of the contest. They who have not gone down into the racecourse do not anoint themselves with oil nor get covered with dust. For those whom glory awaits trouble is at hand. The perfumed spectators are wont to look on, not to join in the struggle, nor to endure the sun, the heat, the dust, and the showers. Let the athletes say to them: Come, strive with us. The spectators will but answer: We sit here now to decide about you, but you, if you conquer, will gain the glory of the crown and we shall not.

61. They, then, who have devoted themselves to pleasures, luxury, robbery, gain, or honours are spectators rather than combatants. They have the profit of labour, but not the fruits of virtue. They love their ease; by cunning and wickedness they heap up riches; but they will pay the penalty of their iniquity, though it be late. Their rest will be in hell, yours in heaven; their home in the grave, yours in paradise. Whence Job said beautifully that they watch in the tomb, (Job 21:32) for they cannot have the calm of quiet rest which he enjoys who shall rise again.

62. Do not, therefore, understand, or speak, or think as a child; nor as a child claim those things now which belong to a future time. The crown belongs to the perfect. Wait till that which is perfect has come, when you may know— not through a glass as in a riddle, but face to face (1 Corinthians 13:12) — the very form of truth made clear. Then will be made known why that person was rich who was wicked and a robber of other men's goods, why another was powerful, why a third had many children, and yet a fourth was loaded with honours.

63. Perhaps all this happens that the question may be asked of the robber: You were rich, so why did you seize on the goods of others? Need did not force you, poverty did not drive you to it. Did I not make you rich, that you might have no excuse? So, too, it may be said to a person of power: Why did you not aid the widow, the orphans also, when

enduring wrong? Were you powerless? Could you not help? I made you for this purpose, not that you might do wrong, but that you might check it. Is it not written for you Save him that endures wrong? (Sirach 4:9) Is it not written for you: Deliver the poor and needy out of the hand of the sinner? It may be said also to the man who has abundance of good things: I have blessed you with children and honours; I have granted you health of body; why did you not follow my commands? My servant, what have I done to you, or how have I grieved you? Was it not I that gave you children, bestowed honours, granted health to you? Why did you deny me? Why did you suppose that your actions would not come to my knowledge? Why did you accept my gifts, yet despise my commands?

64. We can gather the same from the example of the traitor Judas. He was chosen among the Twelve Apostles, and had charge of the money bag, to lay it out upon the poor, (John 12:6) that it might not seem as though he had betrayed the Lord because he was unhonoured or in want. Wherefore the Lord granted him this office, that He might also be justified in him; he would be guilty of a greater fault, not as one driven to it by wrong done to him, but as one misusing grace.

Chapter 17.

The duties of youth, and examples suitable to that age, are next put forth.

65. Since it has been made sufficiently plain that there will be punishment for wickedness and reward for virtue, let us proceed to speak of the duties which have to be borne in mind from our youth up, that they may grow with our years. A good youth ought to have a fear of God, to be subject to his parents, to give honour to his elders, to preserve his purity; he ought not to despise humility, but should love forbearance and modesty. All these are an ornament to youthful years. For as seriousness is the true grace of an old man, and ardour of a young man, so also is modesty, as though by some gift of nature, well set off in a youth.

66. Isaac feared the Lord, as was indeed but natural in the son of Abraham; being subject also to his father to such an extent that he would not avoid death in opposition to his father's will. (Genesis 22:9) Joseph also, though he dreamed that sun and moon and stars made

obeisance to him, yet was subject to his father's will with ready obedience. (Genesis 37:9) So chaste was he, he would not hear even a word unless it were pure; humble was he even to doing the work of a slave, modest, even to taking flight, enduring, even to bearing imprisonment, so forgiving of wrong as even to repay it with good. Whose modesty was such, that, when seized by a woman, he preferred to leave his garment in her hands in flight, rather than to lay aside his modesty. (Genesis 39:12) Moses, (Exodus 4:10) also, and Jeremiah, (Jeremiah 1:6) chosen by the Lord to declare the words of God to the people, were for avoiding, through modesty, that which through grace they could do.

Chapter 18.

On the different functions of modesty. How it should qualify both speech and silence, accompany chastity, commend our prayers to God, govern our bodily motions; on which last point reference is made to two clerics in language by no means unsuited to its object. Further he proceeds to say that one's gait should be in accordance with that same virtue, and how careful one must be that nothing immodest come forth from one's mouth, or be noticed in one's body. All these points are illustrated with very appropriate examples.

67. Lovely, then, is the virtue of modesty, and sweet is its grace! It is seen not only in actions, but even in our words, so that we may not go beyond due measure in speech, and that our words may not have an unbecoming sound. The mirror of our mind often enough reflects its image in our words. Sobriety weighs out the sound even of our voice, for fear that too loud a voice should offend the ear of any one. Nay, in singing itself the first rule is modesty, and the same is true in every kind of speech, too, so that a man may gradually learn to praise God, or to sing songs, or even to speak, in that the principles of modesty grace his advance.

68. Silence, again, wherein all the other virtues rest, is the chief act of modesty. Only, if it is supposed to be a sign of a childish or proud spirit, it is accounted a reproach; if a sign of modesty, it is reckoned for praise. Susanna was silent in danger, and thought the loss of modesty was worse than loss of life. She did not consider that her safety should be guarded at the risk of her chastity. To God alone she spoke, to Whom she could speak out in true modesty. She avoided looking on the face of men. For there is also modesty in the glance of the eye,

which makes a woman unwilling to look upon men, or to be seen by them.

69. Let no one suppose that this praise belongs to chastity alone. For modesty is the companion of purity, in company with which chastity itself is safer. Shame, again, is good as a companion and guide of chastity, inasmuch as it does not suffer purity to be defiled in approaching even the outskirts of danger. This it is that, at the very outset of her recognition, commends the Mother of the Lord to those who read the Scriptures, and, as a credible witness, declares her worthy to be chosen to such an office. For when in her chamber, alone, she is saluted by the angel, she is silent, and is disturbed at his entrance, and the Virgin's face is troubled at the strange appearance of a man's form. And so, though she was humble, yet it was not because of this, but on account of her modesty, that she did not return his salutation, nor give him any answer, except to ask, when she had learned that she should conceive the Lord, how this should be. She certainly did not speak merely for the sake of making a reply.

70. In our very prayers, too, modesty is most pleasing, and gains us much grace from our God. Was it not this that exalted the publican, and commended him, when he dared not raise even his eyes to heaven? (Luke 18:13-14) So he was justified by the judgment of the Lord rather than the Pharisee, whom overweening pride made so hideous. Therefore let us pray in the incorruptibility of a meek and quiet spirit, which is in the sight of God of great price, (1 Peter 3:4) as St. Peter says. A noble thing, then, is modesty, which, though giving up its rights, seizing on nothing for itself, laying claim to nothing, and in some ways somewhat retiring within the sphere of its own powers, yet is rich in the sight of God, in Whose sight no man is rich. Rich is modesty, for it is the portion of God. Paul also bids that prayer be offered up with modesty and sobriety. (1 Timothy 2:9) He desires that this should be first, and, as it were, lead the way of prayers to come, so that the sinner's prayer may not be boastful, but veiled, as it were, with the blush of shame, may merit a far greater degree of grace, in giving way to modesty at the remembrance of its fault.

71. Modesty must further be guarded in our very movements and gestures and gait. For the condition of the mind is often seen in the attitude of the body. For this reason the hidden man of our heart (our inner self) is considered to be either frivolous, boastful, or boisterous,

or, on the other hand, steady, firm, pure, and dependable. Thus the movement of the body is a sort of voice of the soul.

72. You remember, my children, that a friend of ours who seemed to recommend himself by his assiduity in his duties, yet was not admitted by me into the number of the clergy, because his gestures were too unseemly. Also that I bade one, whom I found already among the clergy, never to go in front of me, because he actually pained me by the seeming arrogance of his gait. That is what I said when he returned to his duty after an offense committed. This alone I would not allow, nor did my mind deceive me. For both have left the Church. What their gait betrayed them to be, such were they proved to be by the faithlessness of their hearts. The one forsook his faith at the time of the Arian troubles; the other, through love of money, denied that he belonged to us, so that he might not have to undergo sentence at the hands of the Church. In their gait was discernible the semblance of fickleness, the appearance, as it were, of wandering buffoons.

73. Some there are who in walking perceptibly copy the gestures of actors, and act as though they were bearers in the processions, and had the motions of nodding statues, to such an extent that they seem to keep a sort of time, as often as they change their step.

74. Nor do I think it becoming to walk hurriedly, except when a case of some danger demands it, or a real necessity. For we often see those who hurry come up panting, and with features distorted. But if there is no reason for the need of such hurry, it gives cause for just offense. I am not, however, talking of those who have to hurry now and then for some particular reason, but of those to whom, by the yoke of constant habit, it has become a second nature. In the case of the former I cannot approve of their slow solemn movements, which remind one of the forms of phantoms. Nor do I care for the others with their headlong speed, for they put one in mind of the ruin of outcasts.

75. A suitable gait is that wherein there is an appearance of authority and weight and dignity, and which has a calm collected bearing. But it must be of such a character that all effort and conceit may be wanting, and that it be simple and plain. Nothing counterfeit is pleasing. Let nature train our movements. If indeed there is any fault in our nature, let us mend it with diligence. And, that artifice may be wanting, let not amendment be wanting.

76. But if we pay so much attention to things like these, how much more careful ought we to be to let nothing shameful proceed out of our mouth, for that defiles a man terribly. It is not food that defiles, but unjust disparagement of others and foul words. These things are openly shameful. In our office indeed must no word be let fall at all unseemly, nor one that may give offense to modesty. But not only ought we to say nothing unbecoming to ourselves, but we ought not even to lend our ears to words of this sort. Thus Joseph fled and left his garment, that he might hear nothing inconsistent with his modesty. (Genesis 39:12) For he who delights to listen, urges the other on to speak.

77. To have full knowledge of what is foul is in the highest degree shameful. To see anything of this sort, if by chance it should happen, how dreadful that is! What, therefore, is displeasing to us in others, can that be pleasing in ourselves? Is not nature herself our teacher, who has formed to perfection every part of our body, so as to provide for what is necessary and to beautify and grace its form? However she has left plain and open to the sight those parts which are beautiful to look upon; among which, the head, set as it were above all, and the pleasant lines of the figure, and the appearance of the face are prominent, while their usefulness for work is ready to hand. But those parts in which there is a compliance with the necessities of nature, she has partly put away and hidden in the body itself, lest they should present a disgusting appearance, and partly, too, she has taught and persuaded us to cover them.

78. Is not nature herself then a teacher of modesty? Following her example, the modesty of men, which I suppose is so called from the mode of knowing what is seemly, has covered and veiled what it has found hid in the frame of our body; like that door which Noah was bidden to make in the side of the ark; (Genesis 6:16) wherein we find a figure of the Church, and also of the human body, for through that door the remnants of food were cast out. Thus the Maker of our nature so thought of our modesty, and so guarded what was seemly and virtuous in our body, as to place what is unseemly behind, and to put it out of the sight of our eyes. Of this the Apostle says well: Those members of the body which seem to be more feeble are necessary, and those members of the body which we think to be less honourable, upon these we bestow more abundant honour, and our uncomely parts have more abundant comeliness. (1 Corinthians 12:22-23) Truly, by following the guidance of nature, diligent care has added to the grace of the body. In

another place I have gone more fully into this subject, and said that not only do we hide those parts which have been given us to hide, but also that we think it unseemly to mention by name their description, and the use of those members.

79. And if these parts are exposed to view by chance, modesty is violated; but if on purpose, it is reckoned as utter shamelessness. Wherefore Ham, Noah's son, brought disgrace upon himself; for he laughed when he saw his father naked, but they who covered their father received the gift of a blessing. (Genesis 9:22) For which cause, also, it was an ancient custom in Rome, and in many other states as well, that grown-up sons should not bathe with their parents, or sons-in-law with their fathers-in-law, in order that the great duty of reverence for parents should not be weakened. Many, however, cover themselves so far as they can in the baths, so that, where the whole body is bare, that part of it at least may be covered.

80. The priests, also, under the old law, as we read in Exodus, wore breeches, as it was told Moses by the Lord: And you shall make them linen breeches to cover their shame: from the loins even to the thighs they shall reach, and Aaron and his sons shall wear them, when they enter into the tabernacle of witness, and when they come unto the altar of the holy place to offer sacrifice, that they lay not sin upon themselves and die. (Exodus 28:42-43) Some of us are said still to observe this, but most explain it spiritually, and suppose it was said with a view to guarding modesty and preserving chastity.

Chapter 19.

How should seemliness be represented by a speaker? Does beauty add anything to virtue, and, if so, how much? Lastly, what care should we take that nothing conceited or effeminate be seen in us?

81. It has given me pleasure to dwell somewhat at length on the various functions of modesty; for I speak to you who either can recognize the good that is in it in your own cases, or at least do not know its loss. Fitted as it is for all ages, persons, times, and places, yet it most beseems youthful and childish years.

82. But at every age we must take care that all we do is seemly and becoming, and that the course of our life forms one harmonious and

complete whole. Wherefore Cicero thinks that a certain order ought to be observed in what is seemly. He says that this lies in beauty, order, and in appointment fitted for action. This, as he says, it is difficult to explain in words, yet it can be quite sufficiently understood.

83. Why Cicero should have introduced beauty, I do not quite understand; though it is true he also speaks in praise of the powers of the body. We certainly do not locate virtue in the beauty of the body, though, on the other hand, we do recognize a certain grace, as when modesty is wont to cover the face with a blush of shame, and to make it more pleasing. For as a workman is wont to work better the more suitable his materials are, so modesty is more conspicuous in the comeliness of the body. Only the comeliness of the body should not be assumed; it should be natural and artless, unstudied rather than elaborated, not heightened by costly and glistening garments, but just clad in ordinary clothing. One must see that nothing is wanting that one's credit or necessity demands, while nothing must be added for the sake of splendour.

84. The voice, too, should not be languid, nor feeble, nor womanish in its tone—such a tone of voice as many are in the habit of using, under the idea of seeming important. It should preserve a certain quality, and rhythm, and a manly vigour. For all to do what is best suited to their character and sex, that is to attain to beauty of life. This is the best order for movements, this the employment fitted for every action. But as I cannot approve of a soft or weak tone of voice, or an effeminate gesture of the body, so also I cannot approve of what is boorish and rustic. Let us follow nature. The imitation of her provides us with a principle of training, and gives us a pattern of virtue.

Chapter 20.
If we are to preserve our modesty we must avoid fellowship with profligate men, also the banquets of strangers, and intercourse with women; our leisure time at home should be spent in pious and virtuous pursuits.

85. Modesty has indeed its rocks— not any that she brings with her, but those, I mean, which she often runs against, as when we associate with profligate men, who, under the form of pleasantry, administer poison to the good. And the latter, if they are very constant in their

attendance at banquets and games, and often join in jests, enervate that manly gravity of theirs. Let us then take heed that, in wishing to relax our minds, we do not destroy all harmony, the blending as it were of all good works. For habit quickly bends nature in another direction.

86. For this reason I think that what ye wisely do is befitting to the duties of clerics, and especially to those of the priesthood— namely, that you avoid the banquets of strangers, but so that you are still hospitable to travellers, and give no occasion for reproach by reason of your great care in the matter. Banquets with strangers engross one's attention, and soon produce a love for feasting. Tales, also, of the world and its pleasures often creep in. One cannot shut one's ears; and to forbid them is looked on as a sign of haughtiness. One's glass, too, even against one's will, is filled time after time. It is better surely to excuse oneself once for all at one's own home, than often at another's. When one rises sober, at any rate one's presence need not be condemned by the insolence of another.

87. There is no need for the younger clergy to go to the houses of widows or virgins, except for the sake of a definite visit, and in that case only with the elder clergy, that is, with the bishop, or, if the matter be somewhat important, with the priests. Why should we give room to the world to revile? What need is there for those frequent visits to give ground for rumours? What if one of those women should by chance fall? Why should you undergo the reproach of another's fall? How many even strong men have been led away by their passions? How many are there who have not indeed yielded to sin, but have given ground for suspicion?

88. Why do you not spend the time which you have free from your duties in the church in reading? Why do you not go back again to see Christ? Why do you not address Him, and hear His voice? We address Him when we pray, we hear Him when we read the sacred oracles of God. What have we to do with strange houses? There is one house which holds all. They who need us can come to us. What have we to do with tales and fables? An office to minister at the altar of Christ is what we have received; no duty to make ourselves agreeable to men has been laid upon us.

89. We ought to be humble, gentle, mild, serious, patient. We must keep the mean in all things, so that a calm countenance and quiet speech may show that there is no vice in our lives.

Chapter 21.

We must guard against anger, before it arises; if it has already arisen we must check and calm it, and if we cannot do this either, at least we should keep our tongue from abuse, so that our passions may be like boys' quarrels. He relates what Archites said, and shows that David led the way in this matter, both in his actions and in his writings.

90. Let anger be guarded against. If it cannot, however, be averted, let it be kept within bounds. For indignation is a terrible incentive to sin. It disorders the mind to such an extent as to leave no room for reason. The first thing, therefore, to aim at, if possible, is to make tranquillity of character our natural disposition by constant practice, by desire for better things, by fixed determination. But since passion is to a large extent implanted in our nature and character, so that it cannot be uprooted and avoided, it must be checked by reason, if, that is, it can be foreseen. And if the mind has already been filled with indignation before it could be foreseen or provided against in any way, we must consider how to conquer the passion of the mind, how to restrain our anger, that it may no more be so filled. Resist wrath, if possible; if not, give way, for it is written: Give place to wrath. (Romans 12:19)

91. Jacob dutifully gave way to his brother when angry, and to Rebecca; that is to say, taught by counsels of patience, he preferred to go away and live in foreign lands, rather than to arouse his brother's anger; and then to return only when he thought his brother was appeased. (Genesis 27:42) Thus it was that he found such great grace with God. With what offers of willing service, with what gifts, did he reconcile his brother to himself again, so that he should not remember the blessing which had been taken away from him, but should only remember the reparation now offered?

92. If, then, anger has got the start, and has already taken possession of your mind, and mounted into your heart, forsake not your ground. Your ground is patience, it is wisdom, it is reason, it is the allaying of indignation. And if the stubbornness of your opponent rouses you, and his perverseness drives you to indignation: if you can not calm your

mind, check at least your tongue. For so it is written: Keep your tongue from evil, and your lips that they speak no guile. Seek peace and pursue it. See the peace of holy Jacob, how great it was! First, then, calm your mind. If you can not do this, put a restraint upon your tongue. Lastly, omit not to seek for reconciliation. These ideas the speakers of the world have borrowed from us, and have set down in their writings. But he who said it first has the credit of understanding its meaning.

93. Let us then avoid or at any rate check anger, so that we may not lose our share of praise, nor yet add to our list of sins. It is no light thing to calm one's anger. It is no less difficult a thing than it is not to be roused at all. The one is an act of our own will, the other is an effect of nature. So quarrels among boys are harmless, and have more of a pleasant than a bitter character about them. And if boys quickly come to quarrel one with the other, they are easily calmed down again, and quickly come together with even greater friendliness. They do not know how to act deceitfully and artfully. Do not condemn these children, of whom the Lord says: Unless you are converted and become as this child, you shall not enter into the kingdom of heaven. (Matthew 18:3) So also the Lord Himself, Who is the Power of God, as a Boy, when He was reviled, reviled not again, when He was struck, struck not back. (1 Peter 2:23) Set then your mind on this— like a child never to keep an injury in mind, never to show malice, but that all things may be done blamelessly by you. Regard not the return made you by others. Hold your ground. Guard the simplicity and purity of your heart. Answer not an angry man according to his anger, nor a foolish man according to his folly. One fault quickly calls forth another. If stones are rubbed together, does not fire break forth?

94. The heathen— (they are wont to exaggerate everything in speaking)— make much of the saying of the philosopher Archites of Tarentum, which he spoke to his bailiff: O you wretched man, how I would punish you, if I were not angry. But David already before this had in his indignation held back his armed hand. How much greater a thing it is not to revile again, than not to avenge oneself! The warriors, too, prepared to take vengeance against Nabal, Abigail restrained by her prayers. From whence we perceive that we ought not only to yield to timely entreaties, but also to be pleased with them. So much was David pleased that he blessed her who intervened, because he was restrained from his desire for revenge.

95. Already before this he had said of his enemies: For they cast iniquity upon me, and in their wrath they were grievous to me. Let us hear what he said when overwhelmed in wrath: Who will give me wings like a dove, and I will flee away and be at rest. They kept provoking him to anger, but he sought quietness.

96. He had also said: Be angry and sin not. The moral teacher who knew that the natural disposition should rather be guided by a reasonable course of teaching, than be eradicated, teaches morals, and says: Be angry where there is a fault against which you ought to be angry. For it is impossible not to be roused up by the baseness of many things; otherwise we might be accounted, not virtuous, but apathetic and neglectful. Be angry therefore, so that you keep free from fault, or, in other words: If you are angry, do not sin, but overcome wrath with reason. Or one might put it thus: If you are angry, be angry with yourselves, because you are roused, and you will not sin. For he who is angry with himself, because he has been so easily roused, ceases to be angry with another. But he who wishes to prove his anger is righteous only gets the more inflamed, and quickly falls into sin. Better is he, as Solomon says, that restrains his anger, than he that takes a city, (Proverbs 16:32) for anger leads astray even brave men.

97. We ought therefore to take care that we do not get into a flurry, before reason prepares our minds. For oftentimes anger or distress or fear of death almost deprives the soul of life, and beats it down by a sudden blow. It is therefore a good thing to anticipate this by reflection, and to exercise the mind by considering the matter. So the mind will not be roused by any sudden disturbance, but will grow calm, being held in by the yoke and reins of reason.

Chapter 22.

On reflection and passion, and on observing propriety of speech, both in ordinary conversation and in holding discussions.

98. There are two kinds of mental motions — those of reflection and of passion. The one has to do with reflection, the other with passion. There is no confusion one with the other, for they are markedly different and unlike. Reflection has to search and as it were to grind out the truth. Passion prompts and stimulates us to do something. Thus by its very nature reflection diffuses tranquillity and calm; and passion sends

forth the impulse to act. Let us then be ready to allow reflection on good things to enter into our mind, and to make passion submit to reason (if indeed we wish to direct our minds to guard what is seemly), lest desire for anything should shut out reason. Rather let reason test and see what befits virtue.

99. And since we have said that we must aim at the observance of what is seemly, so as to know what is the due measure in our words and deeds, and as order in speech rather than in action comes first; speech is divided into two kinds: first, as it is used in friendly conversation, and then in the treatment and discussion of matters of faith and justice. In either case we must take care that there is no irritation. Our language should be mild and quiet, and full of kindness and courtesy and free from insult. Let there be no obstinate disputes in our familiar conversations, for they are wont only to bring up useless subjects, rather than to supply anything useful. Let there be discussion without wrath, urbanity without bitterness, warning without sharpness, advice without giving offense. And as in every action of our life we ought to take heed to this, in order that no overpowering impulse of our mind may ever shut out reason (let us always keep a place for counsel), so, too, ought we to observe that rule in our language, so that neither wrath nor hatred may be aroused, and that we may not show any signs of our greed or sloth.

100. Let our language be of this sort, more especially when we are speaking of the holy Scriptures. For of what ought we to speak more often than of the best subject of conversation, of its exhortation to watchfulness, its care for good instruction? Let us have a reason for beginning, and let our end be within due limits. For a speech that is wearisome only stirs up anger. But surely it is most unseemly that when every kind of conversation generally gives additional pleasure, this should give cause of offense!

101. The treatment also of such subjects as the teaching of faith, instruction on self-restraint, discussion on justice, exhortation to activity, must not be taken up by us and fully gone into all at one time, but must be carried on in course, so far as we can do it, and as the subject-matter of the passage allows. Our discourse must not be too lengthy, nor too soon cut short, for fear the former should leave behind it a feeling of aversion, and the latter produce carelessness and neglect. The address should be plain and simple, clear and evident, full of dignity

and weight; it should not be studied or too refined, nor yet, on the other hand, be unpleasing and rough in style.

Chapter 23.

Jests, although at times they may be quite proper, should be altogether banished among clerics. The voice should be plain and frank.

102. Men of the world give many further rules about the way to speak, which I think we may pass over; as, for instance, the way jesting should be conducted. For though at times jests may be proper and pleasant, yet they are unsuited to the clerical life. For how can we adopt those things which we do not find in the holy Scriptures?

103. We must also take care that in relating stories we do not alter the earnest purpose of the harder rule we have set before us. Woe unto you that laugh, for you shall weep, (Luke 6:25) says the Lord. Do we seek for something to laugh at, that laughing here we may weep hereafter? I think we ought to avoid not only broad jokes, but all kinds of jests, unless perchance it is not unfitting at the time for our conversation to be agreeable and pleasant.

104. In speaking of the voice, I certainly think it ought to be plain and clear. That it should be musical is a gift of nature, and is not to be won by exertion. Let it be distinct in its pronunciation and full of a manly vigour, but let it be free from a rough and rustic twang. See, too, that it does not assume a theatrical accent, but rather keeps true to the inner meaning of the words it utters.

Chapter 24.

There are three things to be noticed in the actions of our life. First, our passions are to be controlled by our reason; next, we ought to observe a suitable moderation in our desires; and, lastly, everything ought to be done at the right time and in the proper order. All these qualities shone forth so conspicuously in the holy men of Old Testament time, that it is evident they were well furnished with what men call the cardinal virtues.

105. I think I have said enough on the art of speaking. Let us now consider what beseems an active life. We note that there are three things

to be regarded in connection with this subject. One is, that passion should not resist our reason. In that way only can our duties be brought into line with what is seemly. For if passion yields to reason we can easily maintain what is seemly in our duties. Next, we must take care lest, either by showing greater zeal or less than the matter we take up demands, we look as though we were taking up a small matter with great parade or were treating a great matter with but little care. Thirdly, as regards moderation in our endeavours and works, and also with regard to order in doing things and in the right timing of things, I think that everything should be open and straightforward.

106. But first comes that which I may call the foundation of all, namely, that our passions should obey our reason. The second and third are really the same— moderation in either case. There is room with us for the survey of a pleasing form, which is accounted beauty, and the consideration of dignity. Next follows the consideration of the order and the timing of things. These, then, are the three points, and we must see whether we can show them in perfection in any one of the saints.

107. First there is our father Abraham, who was formed and called for the instruction of generations to come. When bidden to go forth from his own country and kindred and from his father's house, though bound and held back by many ties of relationship, did he not give proof that in him passion was subject to reason? Who does not delight in the sweet charms of his native land, his kindred, and his own home? Their sweetness then delighted him. But the thought of the heavenly command and of an eternal reward influenced him more. Did he not reflect that he could not take his wife with him without the greatest danger, unused as she was to hardships, and so tender to bear insults, and so beautiful as to be likely to arouse the lust of profligate men? Yet he decided somewhat deliberately to undergo all this rather than to escape it by making excuses. Lastly, when he had gone into Egypt, he advised her to say she was his sister, not his wife.

108. See here what passions are at work! He feared for the chastity of his wife, he feared for his own safety, he had his suspicions about the lust of the Egyptians, and yet the reasonableness of performing his duty to God prevailed with him. For he thought that by the favour of God he could be safe everywhere, but if he offended the Lord he could

not abide unharmed even at home. Thus reason conquered passion, and brought it into subjection to itself.

109. When his nephew was taken captive, (Genesis 14:14) without being terrified or dismayed at the hordes of so many kings, he resumed the war. And after the victory was gained he refused his share of the spoil, which he himself had really won. Also, when a son was promised him, though he thought of the lost vigour of his body, now as good as dead, and the barrenness of his wife, and his own great age, he believed God, though it was against the law of nature.

110. Note how everything meets together here. Passion was not wanting, but it was checked. Here was a mind equable in action, which neither treated great things as unimportant or little things as great. Here there was moderation in different affairs, order in things, fitness of occasion, due measure in words. He was foremost in faith, conspicuous in virtue, vigorous in battle, in victory not greedy, at home hospitable, and to his wife attentive.

111. Jacob also, his holy grandson, loved to pass his time at home free from danger; but his mother wished him to live in foreign parts, and so give place to his brother's anger. Sound counsels prevailed over natural feelings. An exile from home, banished from his parents, yet everywhere, in all he did, he observed due measure, such as was fitting, and made use of his opportunities at the right time. So dear was he to his parents at home, that the one, moved by the promptness of his compliance, gave him his blessing, the other inclined towards him with tender love. In the judgment of his brother, also, he was placed first, when he thought that he ought to give up his food to his brother. For though according to his natural inclinations he wished for food, yet when asked for it he gave it up from a feeling of brotherly affection. He was a faithful shepherd of the flock for his master, an attentive son-in-law to his father-in-law; he was active in work, sparing in his meals, conspicuous in making amends, lavish in repaying. Nay, so well did he calm his brother's anger that he received his favour, though he had feared his enmity. (Genesis 33:4)

112. What shall I say of Joseph? Genesis xxxix He certainly had a longing for freedom, and yet endured the bonds of servitude. How meek he was in slavery, how unchanging in virtue, how kindly in prison! Wise, too, in interpreting, and self-restrained in exercising his

power! In the time of plenty was he not careful? In the time of famine was he not fair? Did he not praiseworthily do everything in order, and use opportunities at their season; giving justice to his people by the restraining guidance of his office?

113. Job also, both in prosperity and adversity, was blameless, patient, pleasing, and acceptable to God. He was harassed with pain, yet could find consolation.

114. David also was brave in war, patient in time of adversity, peaceful at Jerusalem, in the hour of victory merciful, on committing sin repentant, in his old age foreseeing. He preserved due measure in his actions, and took his opportunities as they came. He has set them down in the songs of succeeding years; and so it seems to me that he has by his life no less than by the sweetness of his hymns poured forth an undying song of his own merits to God.

115. What duty connected with the chief virtues was wanting in these men? In the first place they showed prudence, which is exercised in the search of the truth, and which imparts a desire for full knowledge; next, justice, which assigns each man his own, does not claim another's, and disregards its own advantage, so as to guard the rights of all; thirdly, fortitude, which both in warfare and at home is conspicuous in greatness of mind and distinguishes itself in the strength of the body; fourthly, temperance, which preserves the right method and order in all things that we think should either be done or said.

Chapter 25.

A reason is given why this book did not open with a discussion of the above-mentioned virtues. It is also concisely pointed out that the same virtues existed in the ancient fathers.

116. Perhaps, as the different classes of duties are derived from these four virtues, some one may say that they ought to have been described first of all. But it would have been artificial to have given a definition of duty at the outset, and then to have gone on to divide it up into various classes. We have avoided what is artificial, and have put forward the examples of the fathers of old. These certainly offer us no uncertainty as regards our understanding them, and give us no room for subtlety in our discussion of them. Let the life of the fathers, then, be

for us a mirror of virtue, not a mere collection of shrewd and clever acts. Let us show reverence in following them, not mere cleverness in discussing them.

117. Prudence held the first place in holy Abraham. For of him the Scriptures say: Abraham believed God, and that was counted to him for righteousness; (Genesis 15:6) for no one is prudent who knows not God. Again: The fool has said, There is no God; for a wise man would not say so. How is he wise who looks not for his Maker, but says to a stone: You are my father? (Jeremiah 2:27) Who says to the devil as the Manichæan does: You are the author of my being? How is Arius wise, who prefers an imperfect and inferior creator to one who is a true and perfect one? How can Marcion or Eunomius be wise, who prefer to have an evil rather than a good God? And how can he be wise who does not fear his God? For: The fear of the Lord is the beginning of wisdom. Elsewhere, too, it stands: The wise turn not aside from the mouth of the Lord, but come near Him in their confession of His greatness. So when the Scripture says: It was counted to him for righteousness, that brought to him the grace of another virtue.

118. The chief among ourselves have stated that prudence lies in the knowledge of the truth. But who of them all excelled Abraham, David, or Solomon in this? Then they go on to say that justice has regard to the whole community of the human race. So David said: He has dispersed abroad and given to the poor, His righteousness remains for ever. The just man has pity, the just man lends. The whole world of riches lies at the feet of the wise and the just. The just man regards what belongs to all as his own, and his own as common property. The man just accuses himself rather than others. For he is just who does not spare himself, and who does not suffer his secret actions to be concealed. See now how just Abraham was! In his old age he begot a son according to promise, and when the Lord demanded him for sacrifice he did not think he ought to refuse him, although he was his only son. (Genesis 22:3)

119. Note here all these four virtues in one act. It was wise to believe God, and not to put love for his son before the commands of his Creator. It was just to give back what had been received. It was brave to restrain natural feelings by reason. The father led the victim; the son asked where it was: the father's feelings were hardly tried, but were not overcome. The son said again: My father, and thus pierced his fa-

ther's heart, though without weakening his devotion to God. The fourth virtue, temperance, too, was there. Being just he preserved due measure in his piety, and order in all he had to carry out. And so in bringing what was needed for the sacrifice, in lighting the fire, in binding his son, in drawing the knife, in performing the sacrifice in due order; thus he merited as his reward that he might keep his son.

120. Is there greater wisdom than holy Jacob's, who saw God face to face and won a blessing? (Genesis 32:29-30) Can there be higher justice than his in dividing with his brother what he had acquired, and offering it as a gift? (Genesis 33:8) What greater fortitude than his in striving with God? (Genesis 32:24-26) What moderation so true as his, who acted with such moderation as regards time and place, as to prefer to hide his daughter's shame rather than to avenge himself? (Genesis 34:5) For being set in the midst of foes, he thought it better to gain their affections than to concentrate their hate on himself.

121. How wise also was Noah, who built the whole of the ark! (Genesis 6:14) How just again! For he alone, preserved of all to be the father of the human race, was made a survivor of past generations, and the author of one to come; he was born, too, rather for the world and the universe than for himself. How brave he was to overcome the flood! How temperate to endure it! When he had entered the ark, with what moderation he passed the time! When he sent forth the raven and the dove, when he received them on their return, when he took the opportunity of leaving the ark, with what moderation did he make use of these occasions!

Chapter 26.

In investigating the truth the philosophers have broken through their own rules. Moses, however, showed himself more wise than they. The greater the dignity of wisdom, the more earnestly must we strive to gain it. Nature herself urges us all to do this.

122. It is said, therefore, that in investigating the truth, we must observe what is seemly. We ought to look for what is true with the greatest care. We must not put forward falsehood for truth, nor hide the truth in darkness, nor fill the mind with idle, involved, or doubtful matters. What so unseemly as to worship a wooden thing, which men themselves have made? What shows such darkness as to discuss sub-

jects connected with geometry and astronomy (which they approve of), to measure the depths of space, to shut up heaven and earth within the limits of fixed numbers, to leave aside the grounds of salvation and to seek for error?

123. Moses, learned as he was in all the wisdom of the Egyptians, (Acts 7:22) did not approve of those things, but thought that kind of wisdom both harmful and foolish. Turning away therefrom, he sought God with all the desire of his heart, and thus saw, questioned, heard Him when He spoke. (Exodus 3:4) Who is more wise than he whom God taught, and who brought to nought all the wisdom of the Egyptians, and all the powers of their craft by the might of his works? He did not treat things unknown as well known, and so rashly accept them. Yet these philosophers, though they do not consider it contrary to nature, nor shameful for themselves to worship, and to ask help from an idol which knows nothing, teach us that these two things mentioned in the words just spoken, which are in accordance both with nature and with virtue, ought to be avoided.

124. The loftier the virtue of wisdom is, the more I say we ought to strive for it, so that we may be able to attain to it. And that we may have no ideas which are contrary to nature, or are disgraceful, or unfitting, we ought to give two things, that is, time and care, to considering matters for the sake of investigating them. For there is nothing in which man excels all other living creatures more than in the fact that he has reason, seeks out the origin of things, thinks that the Author of his being should be searched out. For in His hand is our life and death; He rules this world by His nod. And to Him we know that we must give a reason for our actions. For there is nothing which is more of a help to a good life than to believe that He will be our judge, Whom hidden things do not escape, and unseemly things offend, and good deeds delight.

125. In all men, then, there lies, in accordance with human nature, a desire to search out the truth, which leads us on to have a longing for knowledge and learning, and infuses into us a wish to seek after it. To excel in this seems a noble thing to mankind; but there are only few who attain to it. And they, by deep thought, by careful deliberation, spend no little labour so as to be able to attain to that blessed and virtuous life, and to approach its likeness in their actions. For not he that says to Me Lord, Lord, shall enter into the kingdom of heaven, but he

that does those things that I say. (Matthew 7:21) To have a desire for knowledge without actions to correspond— well! I do not know whether that carries anything more with it.

Chapter 27.

The first source of duty is prudence, from whence spring three other virtues; and they cannot be separated or torn asunder, since they are mutually connected one with the other.

126. The first source of duty, then, is prudence. For what is more of a duty than to give to the Creator all one's devotion and reverence? This source, however, is drawn off into other virtues. For justice cannot exist without prudence, since it demands no small amount of prudence to see whether a thing is just or unjust. A mistake on either side is very serious. For he that says a just man is unjust, or an unjust man is just, is accursed with God. Wherefore does justice abound unto the wicked? says Solomon. Nor, on the other hand, can prudence exist without justice, for piety towards God is the beginning of understanding. On which we notice that this is a borrowed rather than an original idea among the worldly wise, for piety is the foundation of all virtues.

127. But the piety of justice is first directed towards God; secondly, towards one's country; next, towards parents; lastly, towards all. This, too, is in accordance with the guidance of nature. From the beginning of life, when understanding first begins to be infused into us, we love life as the gift of God, we love our country and our parents; lastly, our companions, with whom we like to associate. Hence arises true love, which prefers others to self, and seeks not its own, wherein lies the pre-eminence of justice.

128. It is ingrained in all living creatures, first of all, to preserve their own safety, to guard against what is harmful, to strive for what is advantageous. They seek food and converts, whereby they may protect themselves from dangers, storms, and sun—all which is a mark of prudence. Next we find that all the different creatures are by nature wont to herd together, at first with fellows of their own class and sort, then also with others. So we see oxen delighted to be in herds, horses in droves, and especially like with like, stags, also, in company with stags and often with men. And what should I say on their desire to

have young, and on their offspring, or even on their passions, wherein the likeness of justice is conspicuous?

129. It is clear, then, that these and the remaining virtues are related to one another. For courage, which in war preserves one's country from the barbarians, or at home defends the weak, or comrades from robbers, is full of justice; and to know on what plan to defend and to give help, how to make use of opportunities of time and place, is the part of prudence and moderation, and temperance itself cannot observe due measure without prudence. To know a fit opportunity, and to make return according to what is right, belongs to justice. In all these, too, large-heartedness is necessary, and fortitude of mind, and often of body, so that we may carry out what we wish.

Chapter 28.

A community rests upon justice and good-will. Two parts of the former, revenge and private possession, are not recognized by Christians. What the Stoics say about common property and mutual help has been borrowed from the sacred writings. The greatness of the glory of justice, and what hinders access to it.

130. Justice, then, has to do with the society of the human race, and the community at large. For that which holds society together is divided into two parts—justice and good-will, which also is called liberality and kindness. Justice seems to me the loftier, liberality the more pleasing, of the two. The one gives judgment, the other shows goodness.

131. But that very thing is excluded with us which philosophers think to be the office of justice. For they say that the first expression of justice is, to hurt no one, except when driven to it by wrongs received. This is put aside by the authority of the Gospel. For the Scripture wills that the Spirit of the Son of Man should be in us, Who came to give grace, not to bring harm. (Luke 9:56)

132. Next they considered it consonant with justice that one should treat common, that is, public property as public, and private as private. But this is not even in accord with nature, for nature has poured forth all things for all men for common use. God has ordered all things to be produced, so that there should be food in common to all, and that the

Book One

earth should be a common possession for all. Nature, therefore, has produced a common right for all, but greed has made it a right for a few. Here, too, we are told that the Stoics taught that all things which are produced on the earth are created for the use of men, but that men are born for the sake of men, so that mutually one may be of advantage to another.

133. But whence have they got such ideas but out of the holy Scriptures? For Moses wrote that God said: Let us make man in our image, after our likeness, and let them have dominion over the fish of the sea, and over the fowl of the air, and over the cattle, and over every creeping thing that creeps upon the earth. (Genesis 1:26) And David said: You have put all things under his feet; all sheep and oxen, yea, and the beasts of the field, the fowls of the air, and the fishes of the sea. So these philosophers have learned from our writings that all things were made subject to man, and, therefore, they think that all things were produced also for man's sake.

134. That man was made for the sake of man we find stated also in the books of Moses, when the Lord says: It is not good that man should be alone, let us make him an helpmeet for him. (Genesis 2:18) Thus the woman was given to the man to help him. She should bear him children, that one man might always be a help to another. Again, before the woman was formed, it was said of Adam: There was not found an help-meet for him. (Genesis 2:20) For one man could not have proper help but from another. Amongst all the living creatures, therefore, there was none meet for him, or, to put it plainly, none to be his helper. Hence a woman was looked for to help him.

135. Thus, in accordance with the will of God and the union of nature, we ought to be of mutual help one to the other, and to vie with each other in doing duties, to lay all our advantages as it were before all, and (to use the words of Scripture) to bring help one to the other from a feeling of devotion or of duty, by giving money, or by doing something, at any rate in some way or other; so that the charm of human fellowship may ever grow sweeter among us, and none may ever be recalled from their duty by the fear of danger, but rather account all things, whether good or evil, as their own concern. Thus holy Moses feared not to undertake terrible wars for his people's sake, nor was he afraid of the arms of the mightiest kings, nor yet was he frightened at

the savagery of barbarian nations. He put on one side the thought of his own safety so as to give freedom to the people.

136. Great, then, is the glory of justice; for she, existing rather for the good of others than of self, is an aid to the bonds of union and fellowship among us. She holds so high a place that she has all things laid under her authority, and further can bring help to others and supply money; nor does she refuse her services, but even undergoes dangers for others.

137. Who would not gladly climb and hold the heights of this virtue, were it not that greed weakens and lessens the power of such a virtue? For as long as we want to add to our possessions and to heap up money, to take into our possession fresh lands, and to be the richest of all, we have cast aside the form of justice and have lost the blessing of kindness towards all. How can he be just that tries to take from another what he wants for himself?

138. The desire to gain power also enervates the perfect strength and beauty of justice. For how can he, who attempts to bring others under his own power, come forward on behalf of others? And how can a man help the weak against the strong, when he himself aspires to great power at the cost of liberty?

Chapter 29.

Justice should be observed even in war and with enemies. This is proved by the example of Moses and Elisha. The ancient writers learned in turn from the Hebrews to call their enemies by a gentler term. Lastly, the foundation of justice rests on faith, and its symmetry is perfect in the Church.

139. How great a thing justice is can be gathered from the fact that there is no place, nor person, nor time, with which it has nothing to do. It must even be preserved in all dealings with enemies. For instance, if the day or the spot for a battle has been agreed upon with them, it would be considered an act against justice to occupy the spot beforehand, or to anticipate the time. For there is some difference whether one is overcome in some battle by a severe engagement, or by superior skill, or by a mere chance. But a deeper vengeance is taken on fiercer foes, and on those that are false as well as on those who have done

greater wrongs, as was the case with the Midianites. (Numbers xxxi) For they had made many of the Jewish people to sin through their women; for which reason the anger of the Lord was poured out upon the people of our fathers. Thus it came about that Moses when victorious allowed none of them to live. On the other hand, Joshua did not attack the Gibeonites, who had tried the people of our fathers with guile rather than with war, but punished them by laying on them a law of bondage. (Joshua ix) Elisha again would not allow the king of Israel to slay the Syrians when he wished to do so. He had brought them into the city, when they were besieging him, after he had struck them with instantaneous blindness, so that they could not see where they were going. For he said: You shall not smite those whom you have not taken captive with your spear and with your sword. Set before them bread and water, that they may eat and drink and return and go to their own home. Incited by their kind treatment they should show forth to the world the kindness they had received. Thus (we read) there came no more the bands of Syria into the land of Israel.

140. If, then, justice is binding, even in war, how much more ought we to observe it in time of peace. Such favour the prophet showed to those who came to seize him. We read that the king of Syria had sent his army to lie in wait for him, for he had learned that it was Elisha who had made known to all his plans and consultations. And Gehazi the prophet's servant, seeing the army, began to fear that his life was in danger. But the prophet said to him: Fear not, for they that be with us are more than they that be with them. And when the prophet asked that the eyes of his servant might be opened, they were opened. Then Gehazi saw the whole mountain full of horses and chariots round about Elisha. As they came down to him the prophet says: Smite, O God, the army of Syria with blindness. And this prayer being granted, he says to the Syrians: Follow me, and I will bring you to the man whom you seek. Then saw they Elisha, whom they were endeavouring to lay hold of, and seeing him they could not hold him fast. It is clear from this that faith and justice should be observed even in war; and that it could not but be a disgraceful thing if faith were violated.

141. So also the ancients used to give their foes a less harsh name, and called them strangers. For enemies used to be called strangers after the customs of old. This too we can say they adopted from our writings; for the Hebrews used to call their foes allophyllos, that is, when put into Latin, alienigenas (of another race). For so we read in the first

book of Kings: It came to pass in those days that they of another race put themselves in array against Israel.

142. The foundation of justice therefore is faith, for the hearts of the just dwell on faith, and the just man that accuses himself builds justice on faith, for his justice becomes plain when he confesses the truth. So the Lord says through Isaiah: Behold, I lay a stone for a foundation in Sion. (Isaiah 28:16) This means Christ as the foundation of the Church. For Christ is the object of faith to all; but the Church is as it were the outward form of justice, she is the common right of all. For all in common she prays, for all in common she works, in the temptations of all she is tried. So he who denies himself is indeed a just man, is indeed worthy of Christ. For this reason Paul has made Christ to be the foundation, so that we may build upon Him the works of justice, (1 Corinthians 3:11) while faith is the foundation. In our works, then, if they are evil, there appears unrighteousness; if they are good, justice.

Chapter 30.

On kindness and its several parts, namely, good-will and liberality. How they are to be combined. What else is further needed for any one to show liberality in a praiseworthy manner.

143. Now we can go on to speak of kindness, which breaks up into two parts, goodwill and liberality. Kindness to exist in perfection must consist of these two qualities. It is not enough just to wish well; we must also do well. Nor, again, is it enough to do well, unless this springs from a good source even from a good will. For God loves a cheerful giver. (2 Corinthians 9:7) If we act unwillingly, what is our reward? Wherefore the Apostle, speaking generally, says: If I do this thing willingly, I have a reward, but if unwillingly, a dispensation is given unto me. (1 Corinthians 9:17) In the Gospel, also, we have received many rules of just liberality.

144. It is thus a glorious thing to wish well, and to give freely, with the one desire to do good and not to do harm. For if we were to think it our duty to give the means to an extravagant man to live extravagantly, or to an adulterer to pay for his adultery, it would not be an act of kindness, for there would be no good-will in it. We should be doing harm, not good, to another if we gave him money to aid him in plotting against his country, or in attempting to get together at our expense

some abandoned men to attack the Church. Nor, again, does it look like liberality to help one who presses very hardly on widows and orphans, or attempts to seize on their property with any show of violence.

145. It is no sign of a liberal spirit to extort from one what we give to another, or to gain money unjustly, and then to think it can be well spent, unless we act as Zacchæus (Luke 19:8) did, and restore fourfold what we have taken from him whom we have robbed, and make up for such heathenish crimes by the zeal of our faith and by true Christian labour. Our liberality must have some sure foundation.

146. The first thing necessary is to do kindness in good faith, and not to act falsely when the offering is made. Never let us say we are doing more, when we are really doing less. What need is there to speak at all? In a promise a cheat lies hid. It is in our power to give what we like. Cheating shatters the foundation, and so destroys the work. Did Peter grow angry only so far as to desire that Ananias and his wife should be slain? (Acts 5:11) Certainly not. He wished that others, through knowing their example, should not perish.

147. Nor is it a real act of liberality if you give for the sake of boasting about it, rather than for mercy's sake. Your inner feelings give the name to your acts. As it comes forth from you, so will others regard it. See what a true judge you have! He consults with you how to take up your work, and first of all he questions your mind. Let not, he says, your left hand know what your right hand does. (Matthew 6:3) This does not refer to our actual bodies, but means: Let not him who is of one mind with you, not even your brother, know what you do, lest you should lose the fruit of your reward hereafter by seeking here your price in boastfulness. But that liberality is real where a man hides what he does in silence, and secretly assists the needs of individuals, whom the mouth of the poor, and not his own lips, praises.

148. Perfect liberality is proved by its good faith, the case it helps, the time and place when and where it is shown. But first we must always see that we help those of the household of faith. (Galatians 6:10) It is a serious fault if a believer is in want, and you know it, or if you know that he is without means, that he is hungry, that he suffer distress, especially if he is ashamed of his need. It is a great fault if he is overwhelmed by the imprisonment or false accusation of his family,

and thou dost not come to his help. If he is in prison, and— upright though he is— has to suffer pain and punishment for some debt (for though we ought to show mercy to all, yet we ought to show it especially to an upright man); if in the time of his trouble he obtains nothing from you; if in the time of danger, when he is carried off to die, your money seems more to you than the life of a dying man; what a sin is that to you! Wherefore Job says beautifully: Let the blessing of him that was ready to perish come upon me. (Job 29:13)

149. God, indeed, is not a respecter of persons, for He knows all things. And we, indeed, ought to show mercy to all. But as many try to get help on false pretences, and make out that they are miserably off; therefore where the case is plain and the person well known, and no time is to be lost, mercy ought to be shown more readily. For the Lord is not exacting to demand the utmost. Blessed, indeed, is he who forsakes all and follows Him, but blessed also is he who does what he can to the best of his powers with what he has. The Lord preferred the two mites of the widow to all the gifts of the rich, for she gave all that she had, but they only gave a small part out of all their abundance. (Luke 21:3-4) It is the intention, therefore, that makes the gift valuable or poor, and gives to things their value. The Lord does not want us to give away all our goods at once, but to impart them little by little; unless, indeed, our case is like that of Elisha, who killed his oxen, and fed the people on what he had, so that no household cares might hold him back, and that he might give up all things, and devote himself to the prophetic teaching.

150. True liberality also must be tested in this way: that we despise not our nearest relatives, if we know they are in want. For it is better for you to help your kindred who feel the shame of asking help from others, or of going to another to beg assistance in their need. Not, however, that they should become rich on what you could otherwise give to the poor. It is the facts of the case we must consider, and not personal feeling. You did not dedicate yourself to the Lord on purpose to make your family rich, but that you might win eternal life by the fruit of good works, and atone for your sins by showing mercy. They think perhaps that they are asking but little, but they demand the price you should pay for your sins. They attempt to take away the fruits of your life, and think they are acting rightly. And one accuses you because you have not made him rich, when all the time he wished to cheat you of the reward of eternal life.

Book One

151. So far we have given our advice, now let us look for our authority. First, then, no one ought to be ashamed of becoming poor after being rich, if this happens because he gives freely to the poor; for Christ became poor when He was rich, that through His poverty He might enrich all. (2 Corinthians 8:9) He has given us a rule to follow, so that we may give a good account of our reduced inheritance; whoever has stayed the hunger of the poor has lightened his distress. Herein I give my advice, says the Apostle, for this is expedient for you, that you should be followers of Christ. (2 Corinthians 8:10) Advice is given to the good, but warnings restrain the wrong-doers. Again he says, as though to the good: For you have begun not only to do, but also to be willing, a year ago. (2 Corinthians 8:10) Both of these, and not only one, is the mark of perfection. Thus he teaches that liberality without good-will, and good-will without liberality, are neither of them perfect. Wherefore he also urges us on to perfection, saying: (2 Corinthians 8:11-15) Now, therefore, perform the doing of it; that as the will to do it was ready enough in you, so also there may be the will to accomplish it out of that which you have. For if the will be ready, it is accepted according to that a man has, and not according to that he has not. But not so that others should have plenty, and you should be in want: but let there be equality—your abundance must now serve for their want, that their abundance may serve for your want; that there may be equality, as it is written: He that gathered much had nothing over, and he that gathered little had no lack. (Exodus 16:18)

152. We notice how the Apostle includes both good-will and liberality, as well as the manner, the fruits of right giving, and the persons concerned. The manner certainly, for he gave advice to those not perfect: For only the imperfect suffer anxiety. But if any priest or other cleric, being unwilling to burden the Church, does not give away all that he has, but does honourably what his office demands, he does not seem to me to be imperfect. I think also that the Apostle here spoke not of anxiety of mind, but rather of domestic troubles.

153. And I think it was with reference to the persons concerned that he said: that your abundance might serve for their want, and their abundance for your want. This means, that the abundance of the people might arouse them to good works, so as to supply the want of food of others; while the spiritual abundance of these latter might assist the want of spiritual merits among the people themselves, and so win them a blessing.

154. Wherefore he gave them an excellent example: He that gathered much had nothing over, and he that gathered little had no lack. That example is a great encouragement to all men to show mercy. For he that possesses much gold has nothing over, for all in this world is as nothing; and he that has little has no lack, for what he loses is nothing already. The whole matter is without loss, for the whole of it is lost already.

155. We can also rightly understand it thus. He that has much, although he does not give away, has nothing over. For however much he gets, he always is in want, because he longs for more. And he who has little has no lack, for it does not cost much to feed the poor. In like manner, too, the poor person that gives spiritual blessings in return for money, although he has much grace, has nothing over. For grace does not burden the mind, but lightens it.

156. It can further be taken in this way: You, O man, have nothing over! For how much have you really received, though it may seem much to you? John, than whom none was greater among those born of woman, yet was less than he who is least in the kingdom of heaven. (Matthew 11:11)

157. Or once more. The grace of God is never superabundant, humanly speaking, for it is spiritual. Who can measure its greatness or its breadth, which one cannot see? Faith, if it were as a grain of mustard seed, can transplant mountains— and more than a grain is not granted you. If grace dwelt fully in you, would you not have to fear lest your mind should begin to be elated at so great a gift? For there are many who have fallen more terribly, from spiritual heights, than if they had never received grace at all from the Lord. And he who has little has no lack, for it is not tangible so as to be divided; and what seems little to him that has is much to him that lacks.

158. In giving we must also take into consideration age and weakness; sometimes, also, that natural feeling of shame, which indicates good birth. One ought to give more to the old who can no longer supply themselves with food by labour. So, too, weakness of body must be assisted, and that readily. Again, if any one after being rich has fallen into want, we must assist, especially if he has lost what he had from no sin of his own, but owing to robbery or banishment or false accusation.

159. Perchance some one may say: A blind man sits here in one place, and people pass him by, while a strong young man often has something given him. That is true; for he comes over people by his importunity. That is not because in their judgment he deserves it, but because they are wearied by his begging. For the Lord speaks in the Gospel of him who had already closed his door; how that when one knocks at his door very violently, he rises and gives what is wanted, because of his importunity. (Luke 11:8)

Chapter 31.

A kindness received should be returned with a freer hand. This is shown by the example of the earth. A passage from Solomon about feasting is adduced to prove the same, and is expounded later in a spiritual sense.

160. It is also right that more regard should be paid to him who has conferred some benefit or gift upon you, if he ever is reduced to want. For what is so contrary to one's duty as not to return what one has received? Nor do I think that a return of equal value should be made, but a greater. One ought to make up for the enjoyment of a kindness one has received from another, to such an extent as to help that person, even to putting an end to his needs. For not to be the better in returning than in conferring a kindness, is to be the inferior; for he who was the first to give was the first in point of time, and also first in showing a kind disposition.

161. Wherefore we must imitate the nature of the earth in this respect, which is wont to return the seed she has received, multiplied a thousand-fold. And so it is written: As a field is the foolish man, and as a vineyard is the man without sense. If you leave him, he will be made desolate. As a field also is the wise man, so as to return the seed given him in fuller measure, as though it had been lent to him on interest. The earth either produces fruits of its own accord, or pays back and restores, what it was entrusted with, in fruitful abundance. In both these ways a return is due from you, when you enter upon the use of your father's possession, that you may not be left to lie as an unfruitful field. It may be that a man can make an excuse for not giving anything, but how can he excuse himself for not returning what was given? It is hardly right not to give anything; it is certainly not right to make no return for kindness done to oneself.

162. Therefore Solomon says well: When you sit to eat at the table of a ruler consider diligently what is before you, and put forth your hand, knowing that it behooves you to make such preparations. But if you are insatiable, be not desirous of his dainties, for they have but a deceptive life. I have written these words as I wish that we all should follow them. It is a good thing to do a service, but he who knows not how to return one is very hard. The earth herself supplies an example of kindliness. She provides fruits of her own accord, which thou did not sow; she also returns many-fold what she has received. It is not right for you to deny knowledge of money paid in to you, and how can it be right to let a service done go without notice? In the book of Proverbs also it is said: that the repayment of kindness has such great power with God, that through it, even in the day of destruction, a man may find grace, though his sins outweigh all else. And why need I bring forward other examples when the Lord Himself promises in the Gospel a fuller reward to the merits of the saints, and exhorts us to do good works, saying: Forgive, and you shall be forgiven; give, and it shall be given unto you; good measure, shaken together and running over, shall men give into your bosom. (Luke 6:37-38)

163. But the feasting that Solomon speaks of has not to do with common food only, but it is to be understood as having to do with good works. For how can the soul be feasted in better wise than on good works; or what can so easily fill the mind of the just as the knowledge of a good work done? What pleasanter food is there than to do the will of God? The Lord has told us that He had this food alone in abundance, as it is written in the Gospel, saying: My food is to do the will of My Father which is in heaven. (John 4:34)

164. In this food let us delight of which the prophet says: Delight thou in the Lord. In this food they delight, who have with wonderful knowledge learned to take in the higher delights; who can know what that delight is which is pure and which can be understood by the mind. Let us therefore eat the bread of wisdom, and let us be filled with the word of God. For the life of man made in the image of God consists not in bread alone, but in every word that comes from God. (Matthew 4:4) About the cup, too, holy Job says, plainly enough: As the earth waits for the rain, so did they for my words. (Job 29:23)

Chapter 32.

After saying what return must be made for the service of the above-mentioned feast, various reasons for repaying kindness are enumerated. Then he speaks in praise of good-will, on its results and its order.

165. It is therefore a good thing for us to be bedewed with the exhortations of the divine Scriptures, and that the word of God should come down upon us like the dew. When, therefore, you sit at the table of that great man, understand who that great man is. Set in the paradise of delight and placed at the feast of wisdom, think of what is put before you! The divine Scriptures are the feast of wisdom, and the single books the various dishes. Know, first, what dishes the banquet offers, then stretch forth your hand, that those things which you read, or which you receive from the Lord your God, you may carry out in action, and so by your duties may show forth the grace that was granted you. Such was the case with Peter and Paul, who in preaching the Gospel made some return to Him Who freely gave them all things. So that each of them might say: By the grace of God I am what I am, and His grace in me was not in vain, but I laboured more abundantly than they all. (1 Corinthians 15:10)

166. One repays the fruit of a service done him, and repays it, gold with gold, silver with silver. Another gives his labour. Another— and I do not know whether he does not do it in fuller measure— gives but the best wishes of his heart. But what if there is no opportunity to make a return at hand? If we wish to return a kindness, more depends on the spirit in which we do it than on the amount of our property, while people will think more of our good-will, than of our power to make a full return. For a kindness done is regarded in the light of what one has. A great thing, therefore, is good-will. For even if it has nothing to give, yet it offers the more, and though there is nothing in its own possession, yet it gives largely to many, and does that, too, without loss to itself, and to the gain of the many. Thus good-will is better than liberality itself. It is richer in character than the other is in gifts; for there are more that need a kindness than there are that have abundance.

167. But good-will also goes in conjunction with liberality, for liberality really starts from it, seeing that the habit of giving comes after the

desire to give. It exists, however, also separate and distinct. For where liberality is wanting, there good-will abides— the parent as it were of all in common, uniting and binding friendships together. It is faithful in counsel, joyful in times of prosperity, and in times of sorrow sad. So it happens that any one trusts himself to the counsels of a man of good-will rather than to those of a wise one, as David did. For he, though he was the more farseeing, agreed to the counsels of Jonathan, who was the younger. Remove good-will out of the reach of men, and it is as though one had withdrawn the sun from the world. For without it men would no longer care to show the way to the stranger, to recall the wanderer, to show hospitality (this latter is no small virtue, for on this point Job praised himself, when he said: At my doors the stranger dwelt not, my gate was open to every one who came), (Job 31:32) nor even to give water from the water that flows at their door, or to light another's candle at their own. Thus good-will exists in all these, like a fount of waters refreshing the thirsty, and like a light, which, shining forth to others, fails not them who have given a light to others from their own light.

168. There is also liberality springing from good-will, that makes one tear up the bond of a debtor which one holds, without demanding any of the debt back from him. Holy Job bids us act thus by his own example. For he that has does not borrow, but he that has not does not put an end to the agreement. Why, then, if you have no need, do you save up for greedy heirs what you can give back immediately, and so get praise for good-will, and that without loss of money?

169. To go to the root of the matter— good-will starts first with those at home, that is with children, parents, brothers, and goes on from one step to another throughout the world. Having started from Paradise, it has filled the world. For God set the feeling of good-will in the man and woman, saying: They shall be one flesh, (Genesis 2:24) and (one may add) one spirit. Wherefore Eve also believed the serpent; for she who had received the gift of good-will did not think there was ill-will.

Chapter 33.

Good-will exists especially in the Church, and nourishes kindred virtues.

170. Good-will expands in the body of the Church, by fellowship in faith, by the bond of baptism, by kinship through grace received, by communion in the mysteries. For all these bonds claim for themselves the name of intimacy, the reverence of children, the authority and religious care of parents, the relationship of brothers. Therefore the bonds of grace clearly point to an increase of good-will.

171. The desire to attain to like virtues also stands one in good stead; just as again good-will brings about a likeness in character. For Jonathan the king's son imitated the gentleness of holy David, because he loved him. Wherefore those words: With the holy you shall be holy, seem not only to be concerned with our ordinary intercourse, but also to have some connection with good-will. The sons of Noah indeed dwelt together, and yet their characters were not at all alike. Esau and Jacob also dwelt together in their father's house, but were very unlike. There was, however, no good-will between them to make the one prefer the other to himself, but rather a rivalry as to which should first get the blessing. Since one was so hard, and the other gentle, good-will could not exist as between such different characters and conflicting desires. Add to this the fact that holy Jacob could not prefer the unworthy in son of his father's house to virtue.

172. But nothing is so harmonious as justice and impartiality. For this, as the comrade and ally of good-will, makes us love those whom we think to be like ourselves. Again, good-will contains also in itself fortitude. For when friendship springs from the fount of good-will it does not hesitate to endure the great dangers of life for a friend. If evils come to me through him, it says, I will bear them. (Sirach 23:31)

Chapter 34.

Some other advantages of goodwill are here enumerated.

173. Good-will also is wont to remove the sword of anger. It is also good-will that makes the wounds of a friend to be better than the willing kisses of an enemy. (Proverbs 27:6) Goodwill again makes many to

become one. For if many are friends, they become one; in whom there is but one spirit and one opinion. We note, too, that in friendship corrections are pleasing. They have their sting, but they cause no pain. We are pierced by the words of blame, but are delighted with the anxiety that good-will shows.

174. To conclude, the same duties are not owed to all. Nor is regard ever paid to persons, though the occasion and the circumstances of the case are generally taken into consideration, so that one may at times have to help a neighbour rather than one's brother. For Solomon also says: Better is a neighbour that is near than a brother far off. (Proverbs 27:10) For this reason a man generally trusts himself to the good-will of a friend rather than to the ties of relationship with his brother. So far does good-will prevail that it often goes beyond the pledges given by nature.

Chapter 35.

On fortitude. This is divided into two parts: as it concerns matters of war and matters at home. The first cannot be a virtue unless combined with justice and prudence. The other depends to a large extent upon endurance.

175. We have discussed fully enough the nature and force of what is virtuous from the standpoint of justice. Now let us discuss fortitude, which (being a loftier virtue than the rest) is divided into two parts, as it concerns matters of war and matters at home. But the thought of warlike matters seems to be foreign to the duty of our office, for we have our thoughts fixed more on the duty of the soul than on that of the body; nor is it our business to look to arms, but rather to the affairs of peace. Our fathers, however, as Joshua, the son of Nun, Jerubbaal, Samson, and David, gained great glory also in war.

176. Fortitude, therefore, is a loftier virtue than the rest, but it is also one that never stands alone. For it never depends on itself alone. Moreover, fortitude without justice is the source of wickedness. For the stronger it is, the more ready is it to crush the weaker, while in matters of war one ought to see whether the war is just or unjust.

177. David never waged war unless he was driven to it. Thus prudence was combined in him with fortitude in the battle. For even when about

to fight single-handed against Goliath, the enormous giant, he rejected the armour with which he was laden. His strength depended more on his own arm than on the weapons of others. Then, at a distance, to get a stronger throw, with one cast of a stone, he slew his enemy. After that he never entered on a war without seeking counsel of the Lord. Thus he was victorious in all wars, and even to his last years was ready to fight. And when war arose with the Philistines, he joined battle with their fierce troops, being desirous of winning renown, while careless of his own safety.

178. But this is not the only kind of fortitude which is worthy of note. We consider their fortitude glorious, who, with greatness of mind, through faith stopped the mouth of lions, quenched the violence of fire, escaped the edge of the sword, out of weakness were made strong. (Hebrews 11:33-34) They did not gain a victory in common with many, surrounded with comrades, and aided by the legions, but won their triumph alone over their treacherous foes by the mere courage of their own souls. How unconquerable was Daniel, who feared not the lions raging round about him. The beasts roared, while he was eating.

Chapter 36.

One of the duties of fortitude is to keep the weak from receiving injury; another, to check the wrong motions of our own souls; a third, both to disregard humiliations, and to do what is right with an even mind. All these clearly ought to be fulfilled by all Christians, and especially by the clergy.

179. The glory of fortitude, therefore, does not rest only on the strength of one's body or of one's arms, but rather on the courage of the mind. Nor is the law of courage exercised in causing, but in driving away all harm. He who does not keep harm off a friend, if he can, is as much in fault as he who causes it. Wherefore holy Moses gave this as a first proof of his fortitude in war. For when he saw a Hebrew receiving hard treatment at the hands of an Egyptian, he defended him, and laid low the Egyptian and hid him in the sand. (Exodus 2:11) Solomon also says: Deliver him that is led to death. (Proverbs 24:11)

180. From whence, then, Cicero and Panætius, or even Aristotle, got these ideas is perfectly clear. For though living before these two, Job had said: I delivered the poor out of the hand of the strong, and I aided

the fatherless for whom there was no helper. Let the blessing of him that was ready to perish come upon me. (Job 29:12-13) Was not he most brave in that he bore so nobly the attacks of the devil, and overcame him with the powers of his mind? Nor have we cause to doubt the fortitude of him to whom the Lord said: Gird up your loins like a man. Put on loftiness and power. Humble every one that does wrong. The Apostle also says: You have a strong consolation. (Hebrews 6:18) He, then, is brave who finds consolation in any grief.

181. And in very truth, rightly is that called fortitude, when a man conquers himself, restrains his anger, yields and gives way to no allurements, is not put out by misfortunes, nor gets elated by good success, and does not get carried away by every varying change as by some chance wind. But what is more noble and splendid than to train the mind, keep down the flesh, and reduce it to subjection, so that it may obey commands, listen to reason, and in undergoing labours readily carry out the intention and wish of the mind?

182. This, then, is the first notion of fortitude. For fortitude of the mind can be regarded in two ways. First, as it counts all externals as very unimportant, and looks on them as rather superfluous and to be despised than to be sought after. Secondly, as it strives after those things which are the highest, and all things in which one can see anything moral (or as the Greeks call it, πρέπον,) with all the powers of the mind. For what can be more noble than to train your mind so as not to place a high value on riches and pleasures and honours, nor to waste all your care on these? When your mind is thus disposed, you must consider how all that is virtuous and seemly must be placed before everything else; and you must so fix your mind upon that, that if anything happens which may break your spirit, whether loss of property, or the reception of fewer honours, or the disparagement of unbelievers, you may not feel it, as though thou were above such things; nay, so that even dangers which menace your safety, if undertaken at the call of justice, may not trouble you.

183. This is the true fortitude which Christ's warrior has, who receives not the crown unless he strives lawfully. (2 Timothy 2:5) Or does that call to fortitude seem to you but a poor one: Tribulation works patience, and patience, experience, and experience, hope? (Romans 5:3-4) See how many a contest there is, yet but one crown! That call none gives, but he who was strengthened in Christ Jesus, and whose flesh had no rest.

Book One

Affliction on all sides, fighting without and fears within. (2 Corinthians 7:5) And though in dangers, in countless labours, in prisons, in deaths — he was not broken in spirit, but fought so as to become more powerful through his infirmities.

184. Think, then, how he teaches those who enter upon their duties in the Church, that they ought to have contempt for all earthly things: If, then, you be dead with Christ from the elements of this world, why do ye act as though living in the world? Touch not, taste not, handle not, which all are to perish with the using. And further: If you then be risen with Christ, seek those things which are above, not those things which are on the earth. (Colossians 3:1-2) And again: Mortify, therefore, your members which are on the earth. (Colossians 3:5) This, indeed, is meant for all the faithful. But you, especially, my son, he urges to despise riches and to avoid profane and old wives fables— allowing nothing but this: Exercise yourself unto godliness, for bodily exercise profits a little, but godliness is profitable unto all things. (1 Timothy 4:8)

185. Let, then, godliness exercise you unto justice, continence, gentleness, that you may avoid childish acts, and that rooted and grounded in grace you may fight the good fight of faith. (1 Timothy 6:12) Entangle not yourself in the affairs of this life, for you are fighting for God. (2 Timothy 2:4) For if he who fights for the emperor is forbidden by human laws to enter upon lawsuits, to do any legal business, or to sell merchandise; how much more ought he who enters upon the warfare of faith to keep from every kind of business, being satisfied with the produce of his own little bit of land, if he has it? If he has not that, let him be content with the pay he will get for his service. Here is a good witness to this fact, who says: I have been young and now am old, yet have I not seen the righteous forsaken, nor his seed begging bread. That is the true rest and temperance of the mind which is not excited by the desire of gain, nor tormented by the fear of want.

Chapter 37.

An even mind should be preserved in adversity as well as in prosperity. However, evil things must be avoided.

186. There is also that true freedom of the mind from vexation which makes us neither give way too much in our griefs, nor be too elated in prosperity. And if they who urge men to undertake the affairs of the

state give such rules, how much more ought we who are called to do duty in the Church, to act thus and do those things which are pleasing to God, so that Christ's power may show itself forth in us. We too must prove ourselves to our Captain, so that our members may be the weapons of justice; not carnal weapons in which sin may reign, but weapons strong for God, whereby sin may be destroyed. Let our flesh die, that in it every sin may die. And as though living again after death, may we rise to new works and a new life.

187. These, then, are the services of fortitude; and full they are of virtuous and seemly duties. But in all that we do we must look to see, not only if it is virtuous, but whether it is possible, so that we may not enter upon anything that we cannot carry out. Wherefore the Lord, to use His own word, wills us to flee in the time of persecution from one city to another; (Matthew 10:23) so that no one, while longing for the crown of martyrdom, may put himself in the way of dangers which possibly the weak flesh or a mind indulged could not bear and endure.

Chapter 38.

We must strengthen the mind against troubles to come, and build it up by looking out for them beforehand. What difficulties there are in doing this.

188. But again, no one must retire through cowardice, or give up his faith from fear of danger. With what grace must the soul be equipped, and the mind trained and taught to stand firm, so as never to be disturbed by any fears, to be broken by any troubles, or to yield to any torments! With what difficulty indeed are they borne! But as all pains seem less in the fear of greater pains, so also, if you dost build up your soul by quiet counsel, and dost determine not to go from your course, and layest before you the fear of divine judgment and the torment of eternal punishment, can you gain endurance of mind.

189. If a man thus prepares himself, he gives signs of great diligence. On the other hand it is a sign of natural ability, if a man by the power of his mind can foresee the future, and put as it were before his eyes what may happen, and decide what he ought to do if it should take place. It may happen, too, that he will think over two or three things at once, which he supposes may come either singly or together, and that

he settles what he will do with them as he thinks will be to the most advantage, in the event of their coming either singly or together.

200. Therefore it is the duty of a brave man not to shut his eyes when anything threatens, but to put it before him and to search it out as it were in the mirror of his mind, and to meet the future with foreseeing thought, for fear he might afterwards have to say: This has come to me because I thought it could not come about. If misfortunes are not looked for beforehand, they quickly get a hold over us. In war an unexpected enemy is with difficulty resisted, and if he finds the others unprepared, he easily overcomes them; so evils unthought of readily break down the soul.

200. In these two points, then, consists the excellency of the soul: so that your soul, trained in good thoughts, and with a pure heart, first, may see what is true and virtuous (for blessed are the pure in heart, for they shall see God), (Matthew 5:8) and may decide that only to be good which is virtuous; and, next, may never be disturbed by business of any kind, nor get tossed about by any desires.

201. Not that this is an easy thing for any one. For what is so difficult as to discern, as though from some watchtower, the resources of wisdom and all those other things, which to most seem so great and noble? Again, what so difficult as to place one's decision on fixed grounds, and to despise what one has decided to be worthless, as of no good? Or, once more, what so difficult, when some misfortune has happened, and it is looked on as something serious and grieving, as to bear it in such a way that one considers it nothing beyond what is natural, when one reads: Naked was I born, naked shall I go forth. What the Lord gave, the Lord has taken away (Job 1:21) (he who said this had lost children and possessions), and to preserve in all things the character of a wise and upright man, as he did who says: As the Lord pleased, so did He. Blessed be the name of the Lord. (Job 1:21) And again: You speak as one of the foolish women speaks. Shall we receive good at the hand of God, and shall we not receive evil? (Job 2:10)

Chapter 39.

One must show fortitude in fighting against all vices, especially against avarice. Holy Job teaches this lesson.

202. Fortitude of soul, then, is not an unimportant thing, nor is it cut off from the other virtues, for it wages war in conjunction with the virtues, and alone defends the beauty of all the virtues, and guards their powers of discernment, and fights against all vices with implacable hate. It is unconquerable as regards labours, brave to endure dangers, stern as against pleasures, hardened against allurements, to which it knows not how to lend an ear, nor, so to speak, to give a greeting. It cares not for money, and flies from avarice as from a plague that destroys all virtue. For nothing is so much opposed to fortitude as when one allows oneself to be overcome by gain. Often when the enemy is repulsed and the hosts of the foe are turned to flight, has the warrior died miserably among those whom he has laid low, while he is busy with the spoils of the fallen; and the legions, while busy with their booty, have called back upon them the enemy that had fled, and so have been robbed of their triumph.

203. Fortitude, then, must repulse so foul a plague and crush it down. It must not let itself be tempted by desires, nor shaken by fear. Virtue stands true to itself and bravely pursues all vices as though they were the poison of virtue. It must repel anger as it were with arms, for it removes counsel far off. It must avoid it as though it were some severe sickness. It must further be on its guard against a desire for glory, which often has done harm when sought for too anxiously, and always when it has been once attained.

204. What of all this was wanting in holy Job, or in his virtue, or what came upon him in the way of vice? How did he bear the distress of sickness or cold or hunger? How did he look upon the dangers which menaced his safety? Were the riches from which so much went to the poor gathered together by plunder? Did he ever allow greed for wealth, or the desire for pleasures, or lusts to rise in his heart? Did ever the unkind disputes of the three princes, or the insults of the slaves, rouse him to anger? Did glory carry him away like some fickle person when he called down vengeance on himself if ever he had hidden even an involuntary fault, or had feared the multitude of the people so as not to confess it in the sight of all? His virtues had no

Book One

point of contact with any vices, but stood firm on their own ground. Who, then, was so brave as holy Job? How can he be put second to any, on whose level hardly one like himself can be placed?

Chapter 40.

Courage in war was not wanting in our forefathers, as is shown by the example of the men of old, especially by the glorious deed of Eleazar.

205. But perhaps renown in war keeps some so bound to itself as to make them think that fortitude is to be found in battle alone, and that therefore I had gone aside to speak of these things, because that was wanting in us. But how brave was Joshua the son of Nun, who in one battle laid low five kings together with their people! Joshua x Again, when he fought against the Gibeonites and feared that night might stop him from gaining the victory, he called out with deep faith and high spirit: (Joshua 10:12) Let the sun stand still; and it stood still until the victory was complete. Gideon with three hundred men gained a triumph over a great nation and a cruel foe. Judges vii Jonathan when a young man showed great courage in battle, and what shall I say about the Maccabees?

206. First, I will speak of the people of our fathers. They were ready to fight for the temple of God and for their rights, and when attacked on the Sabbath day by the craft of the enemy, willingly allowed wounds to be inflicted on their unprotected bodies, rather than to join in the fight, so that they might not defile the Sabbath. They all gladly gave themselves up to death. But the Maccabees thinking that then all the nation would perish, on the Sabbath also, when they were challenged to fight, took vengeance for the death of their innocent brethren. And afterwards when he had been roused by this to fresh exertions, King Antiochus, having begun the war afresh under the leadership of his generals Lysias, Nicanor, and Georgias, was so utterly crushed, together with his Eastern and Assyrian forces, that he left 48,000 lying on the battlefield, slain by an army of but 3,000 men.

207. Mark the courage of the leader, Judas Maccabæus, as exemplified in the character of one of his soldiers. Eleazar, (1 Maccabees 6:43) meeting with an elephant higher than all the rest, and with all the royal trappings upon it, and thinking that the king was on it, ran hastily and threw himself into the midst of the legion; and, casting away his

shield, with both hands he slew those opposed to him until he reached the beast. Then he got beneath it, thrust in his sword and slew it. But the beast in falling crushed Eleazar and so killed him. What courage of mind was his then, first, in that he feared not death, next because, when surrounded by enemies, he was carried by it into the thickest of his foes and penetrated the very centre! Then, despising death, and casting away his shield, he ran beneath the huge beast, wounded it with both his hands, and let it fall upon him. He ran beneath it so as to give a more deadly blow. Enclosed by its fall, rather than crushed, he was buried in his own triumph.

208. Nor was he deceived in his intention though he was deceived by the royal ornaments. For the enemy, startled at such an exhibition of valour, dared not rush upon this single unarmed man, held fast though he was. They were so terrified after the mischance of the slaughter of the beast, that they considered themselves altogether unequal to the valour of one. Nay, King Antiochus, son of Lysias, terrified at the fortitude of one, asked for peace. He had come to the war with 120,000 armed men and with 32 elephants, which glittered and gleamed with the sheen of arms like a line of burning lamps, as the sun rose upon them, marching along one by one, like very mountains for size. Thus Eleazar left peace as the heir of his courage. These are the signs of triumphs.

Chapter 41.

After praising Judas' and Jonathan's loftiness of mind, the constancy of the martyrs in their endurance of tortures, which is no small part of fortitude, is next brought before us.

209. But as fortitude is proved not only by prosperity but also in adversity, let us now consider the death of Judas Maccabæus. For he, after Nicanor, the general of King Demetrius, was defeated, boldly engaged 20,000 of the king's army with 900 men who were anxious to retire for fear of being overcome by so great a multitude, but whom he persuaded to endure a glorious death rather than to retire in disgraceful flight. Let us not leave, he says, any stain upon our glory. Thus, then, engaging in battle after having fought from sunrise till evening, he attacks and quickly drives back the right wing, where he sees the strongest troop of the enemy to be. But while pursuing the fugitives from the rear he gave a chance for a wound to be inflicted.

Book One

(1 Maccabees 9:8) Thus he found the spot of death more full of glory for himself than any triumph.

210. Why need I further mention his brother Jonathan, who fought against the king's force, with but a small troop. (1 Maccabees 11:68) Though forsaken by his men, and left with only two, he retrieved the battle, drove back the enemy, and recalled his own men, who were flying in every direction, to share in his triumph.

211. Here, then, is fortitude in war, which bears no light impress of what is virtuous and seemly upon it, for it prefers death to slavery and disgrace. But what am I to say of the sufferings of the martyrs? Not to go too far abroad, did not the children of Maccabæus gain triumphs over the proud King Antiochus, as great as those of their fathers? The latter in truth were armed, but they conquered without arms. The company of the seven brothers stood unconquered, though surrounded by the legions of the king— tortures failed, tormentors ceased; but the martyrs failed not. One, having had the skin of his head pulled off, though changed in appearance, grew in courage. Another, bidden to put forth his tongue, so that it might be cut off, answered: The Lord hears not only those who speak, for He heard Moses when silent. He hears better the silent thoughts of His own than the voice of all others. Do you fear the scourge of my tongue— and do you not fear the scourge of blood spilt upon the ground? Blood, too, has a voice whereby it cries aloud to God— as it did in the case of Abel.

212. What shall I say of the mother (2 Maccabees 7:20) who with joy looked on the corpses of her children as so many trophies, and found delight in the voices of her dying sons, as though in the songs of singers, noting in her children the tones of the glorious harp of her own heart, and a sweeter harmony of love than any strain of the lute could give?

213. What shall I say of those two-year-old children of Bethlehem, (Matthew 2:16) who received the palm of victory before they felt their natural life within them? What of St. Agnes, who when in danger as regards two great matters, that is, chastity and life, protected her chastity and exchanged life for immortality?

214. And let us not pass by St. Lawrence, who, seeing Xystus his bishop led to martyrdom, began to weep, not at his sufferings but at

the fact that he himself was to remain behind. With these words he began to address him: Where, father, are you going without your son? Where, holy priest, are you hastening without your deacon? Never were you wont to offer sacrifice without an attendant. What are you displeased at in me, my father? Have you found me unworthy? Prove, then, whether you have chosen a fitting servant. To him to whom you have entrusted the consecration of the Saviour's blood, to whom you have granted fellowship in partaking of the Sacraments, to him do you refuse a part in your death? Beware lest your good judgment be endangered, while your fortitude receives its praise. The rejection of a pupil is the loss of the teacher; or how is it that noble and illustrious men gain the victory in the contests of their scholars rather than in their own? Abraham offered his son, Peter sent Stephen on before him! Father, show forth your courage in your son. Offer me whom you have trained, that you, confident in your choice of me, may reach the crown in worthy company.

215. Then Xystus said: I leave you not nor forsake you. Greater struggles yet await you. We as old men have to undergo an easier fight; a more glorious triumph over the tyrant awaits you, a young man. Soon shall you come. Cease weeping; after three days you shall follow me. This interval must come between the priest and his levite. It was not for you to conquer under the eye of your master, as though you needed a helper. Why do you seek to share in my death? I leave to you its full inheritance. Why do you need my presence? Let the weak disciples go before their master, let the brave follow him, that they may conquer without him. For they no longer need his guidance. So Elijah left Elisha. To you I entrust the full succession to my own courage.

216. Such was their contention, and surely a worthy one, wherein priest and attendant strove as to who should be the first to suffer for the name of Christ. When that tragic piece is played, it is said there is great applause in the theatre as Pylades says he is Orestes, while Orestes declares that he is really himself. The former acted as he did, that he might die for Orestes, and Orestes, that he might not allow Pylades to be slain instead of himself. But it was not right that they should live, for each of them was guilty of parricide, the one because he had committed the crime, the other because he had helped in its commission. But here there was nothing to call holy Lawrence to act thus but his love and devotion. However, after three days he was placed upon the gridiron by the tyrant whom he mocked, and was burnt. He said: The

flesh is roasted, turn it and eat. So by the courage of his mind he overcame the power of fire.

Chapter 42.
The powers that be are not needlessly to be irritated. One must not lend one's ears to flattery.

217. I think we must take care, lest in being led on by too great a desire for glory, we should abuse the powers that be, and arouse the minds of the heathen, who are opposed to us, to desire persecution, and excite them to anger. How many do some cause to perish, that they themselves may continue to the end, and overcome their tortures!

218. We must also look to it that we do not open our ears to flatterers. To allow oneself to be smoothed down by flattery seems to be a sign not only of want of fortitude, but a sign of actual cowardice.

Chapter 43.
On temperance and its chief parts, especially tranquillity of mind and moderation, care for what is virtuous, and reflection on what is seemly.

219. As we have spoken of three of the virtues, there remains but the fourth for us to speak of. This is called temperance and moderation; wherein, before all else, tranquillity of mind, the attainment of gentleness, the grace of moderation, regard for what is virtuous, and reflection on what is seemly are sought and looked for.

220. We must keep to a certain order in life, so that a foundation may be laid with our first feelings of modesty, for that is the friend and ally of calmness of mind. Avoiding over-confidence, averse to all excess, it loves sobriety, guards what is honourable, and seeks only what is seemly.

221. Let choice of intercourse come next. Let us link ourselves with older men of approved goodness. For as the companionship of people of our own age is the pleasanter, so that of our elders is the safer. By their guidance and the conduct of their lives they give colour to the character of younger men, and tinge them as it were with the deep

purple of probity. For if they who are ignorant of a locality are very glad to take a journey in the company of skilled guides, how much more ought young men to enter on the path of life, which is new to them, in the company of old men; so that they may not go wrong, and turn aside from the true path of virtue. For nothing is better than to have the same men both to direct us in life, and also to be witnesses of how we live.

222. One must also in every action consider what is suitable for different persons, times, and ages, and what will also be in accordance with the abilities of individuals. For often what befits one does not befit another; one thing suits a youth, another an old man; one thing does in danger, another in good fortune.

223. David danced before the ark of the Lord. Samuel did not dance; yet David was not blamed, while the other was praised. David changed his countenance before the king, whose name was Achish. (1 Samuel 21:13) If he had done this without any fear of being recognized, he would certainly not have escaped the charge of levity. Saul also, surrounded by the company of prophets, himself prophesied. Yet of him alone, as though he were unworthy, was it said: Is Saul also among the prophets? (1 Samuel 19:24)

Chapter 44.

Every one ought to apply himself to the duties suited to his character. Many, however, are hindered by following their fathers' pursuits. Clerics act in a different way.

224. Each one knows his own powers. Therefore let each one apply himself to that which he has chosen as suitable to himself. But he must first consider what will be the consequences. He may know his good points, but he must know his faults also. He must also be a fair judge of himself, so as to aim at what is good and avoid what is bad.

225. One is more fitted for the post of reader, another does better for the singing, a third is more solicitous for exorcising those possessed with an evil spirit, another, again, is held to be more suited to have the charge of the sacred things. All these things a priest should look at. He should give each one that particular duty for which he is best fitted.

For whither each one's bent of mind leads him, or whatever duty befits him, that position or duty is filled with greater grace.

226. But as this is a difficult matter in every state of life, so in our case it is most difficult. For each one is wont to follow his parent's choice in life. Thus those whose fathers were in the army generally enter the army too. And others do the same with regard to the different professions.

227. In the clerical office, however, nothing is more rare than to find a man to follow his father's footsteps, either because the difficulties of the work hold him back, or continence in the uncertain days of youth is too difficult to hold to, or the life seems to be too quiet for the activity of youth. So they turn to those pursuits which are thought to be more showy. Most, indeed, prefer the present to the future. They are fighting for the present, we for the future. Wherefore it follows that the greater the cause in which we are engaged, the more must our attention be devoted to it.

Chapter 45.

On what is noble and virtuous, and what the difference between them is, as stated both in the profane and sacred writers.

228. Let us then hold fast modesty, and that moderation which adds to the beauty of the whole of life. For it is no light thing in every matter to preserve due measure and to bring about order, wherein that is plainly conspicuous which we call decorum, or what is seemly. This is so closely connected with what is virtuous, that one cannot separate the two. For what is seemly is also virtuous— and what is virtuous is seemly. So that the distinction lies rather in the words than in the things themselves. That there is a difference between them we can understand, but we cannot explain it.

229. To make an attempt to get some sort of a distinction between them, we may say that what is virtuous may be compared to the good health and soundness of the body, while what is seemly is, as it were, its comeliness and beauty. And as beauty seems to stand above soundness and health, and yet cannot exist without them, nor be separated from them in any way— for unless one has good health, one cannot have beauty and comeliness— so what is virtuous contains in itself

also what is seemly, so as to seem to start with it, and to be unable to exist without it. What is virtuous, then, is like soundness in all our work and undertaking; what is seemly is, as it were, the outward appearance, which, when joined with what is virtuous, can only be known apart in our thoughts. For though in some cases it seems to stand out conspicuous, yet it has its root in what is virtuous, though the flower is its own. Rooted in this, it flourishes; otherwise it fails and droops. For what is virtue, but to avoid anything shameful as though it were death? And what is the opposite of virtue, except that which brings barrenness and death? If, then, the essence of virtue is strong and vigorous, seemliness will also quickly spring forth like a flower, for its root is sound. But if the root of its purpose is corrupt, nothing will grow out of it.

230. In our writings this is put somewhat more plainly. For David says: The Lord reigns, He is clothed with splendour. And the Apostle says: Walk honestly as in the day. (Romans 13:13) The Greek text has εὐσχημόνως — and this really means: with good clothing, with a good appearance. When God made the first man, He created him with a good figure, with limbs well set, and gave him a very noble appearance. He had not given him remission of sins. But afterwards He, Who came in the form of a servant, and in the likeness of man, renewed him with His Spirit, and poured His grace into his heart, and put on Himself the splendour of the redemption of the human race. Therefore the Prophet said: The Lord reigns, He is clothed with splendour. And again he says: A hymn beseems You, O God, in Sion. That is: It is right and good to fear You, to love You, to pray to You, to honour You, for it is written: Let all things be done decently and in order. (1 Corinthians 14:40) But we can also fear, love, ask, honour men; yet the hymn especially is addressed to God. This seemliness which we offer to God we may believe to be far better than other things. It befits also a woman to pray in an orderly dress, (1 Timothy 2:9-10) but it especially beseems her to pray covered, and to pray giving promise of purity together with a good conversation.

Book One

Chapter 46.

A twofold division of what is seemly is given. Next it is shown that what is according to nature is virtuous, and what is otherwise must be looked on as shameful. This division is explained by examples.

231. Seemliness, therefore, which stands conspicuous has a twofold division. For there is what we may call a general seemliness, which is diffused through all that is virtuous, and is seen, as one may say, in the whole body. It is also individual, and shows itself clearly in some particular part. The first has a consistent form and the perfection of what is virtuous harmonizing in every action. For all its life is consistent with itself, and there is no discrepancy in anything. The other is concerned when there is any special action done in a virtuous course of life.

232. At the same time let us note that it is seemly to live in accordance with nature, and to pass our time in accordance with it, and that whatever is contrary to nature is shameful. For the Apostle asks: Is it comely that a woman pray unto God uncovered; does not nature itself teach you that if a man have long hair, it is a shame unto him? For it is contrary to nature. And again he says: If a woman have long hair, it is a glory unto her. (1 Corinthians 11:13-14) It is according to nature, since her hair is given her for a veil, for it is a natural veil. Thus nature arranges for us both character and appearance, and we ought to observe her directions. Would that we could guard her innocence, and not change what we have received by our wickedness!

233. We have that general seemliness; for God made the beauty of this world. We have it also in its parts; for when God made the light, and marked off the day from the night, when He made heaven, and separated land and seas, when He set the sun and moon and stars to shine on the earth, He approved of them all one by one. Therefore this comeliness, which shone forth in each single part of the world, was resplendent in the whole, as the Book of Wisdom shows, saying: I existed, in whom He rejoiced when He was glad at the completion of the world. Likewise also in the building up of the human body each single member is pleasing, but the right adjustment of the members all together delights us far more. For thus they seem to be united and fitted in one harmonious whole.

Chapter 47.

What is seemly should always shine forth in our life. What passions, then, ought we to allow to come to a head, and which should we restrain?

234. If any one preserves an even tenor in the whole of life, and method in all that he does, and sees there is order and consistency in his words and moderation in his deeds, then what is seemly stands forth conspicuous in his life and shines forth as in some mirror.

235. There should be besides a pleasant way of speaking, so that we may win the good-will of those who hear us, and make ourselves agreeable to all our friends and fellow citizens, if possible. Let none show himself to be given to flattery, nor to be desirous of flattery from any one. The one is a mark of artfulness, the other of vanity.

236. Let no one ever look down on what another, least of all a good man, thinks of him, for thus he learns to give regard to the good. For to disregard the judgment of good men is a sign of conceitedness or of weakness. One of these arises from pride, the other from carelessness.

237. We must also guard against the motions of our soul. The soul must always watch and look after itself, so as to guard itself against itself. For there are motions in which there is a kind of passion that breaks forth as it were in a sort of rush. Wherefore in Greek it is called ὁρμή, because it comes out suddenly with some force. In these there lies no slight force of soul or of nature. Its force, however, is twofold: on the one side it rests on passion, on the other on reason, which checks passion, and makes it obedient to itself, and leads it whither it will; and trains it by careful teaching to know what ought to be done, and what ought to be avoided, so as to make it submit to its kind tamer.

238. For we ought to be careful never to do anything rashly or carelessly, or anything at all for which we cannot give a reasonable ground. For though a reason for our action is not given to every one, yet everybody looks into it. Nor, indeed, have we anything whereby we can excuse ourselves. For though there is a sort of natural force in every passion of ours, yet that same passion is subject to reason by the law of nature itself, and is obedient to it. Wherefore it is the duty of a

careful watchman so to keep a lookout, that passion may not outrun reason nor utterly forsake it, lest by outstripping it confusion be caused, and reason be shut out, and come to nothing by such desertion. Disquiet destroys consistency. Withdrawal shows cowardice and implies indolence. For when the mind is disquieted passion spreads wide and far, and in a fierce outburst endures not the reins of reason and feels not the management of its driver so as to be turned back. Wherefore as a rule not only is the soul perturbed and reason lost, but one's countenance gets inflamed by anger or by lust. it grows pale with fear, it contains not itself in pleasure, and cannot bear joy.

239. When this happens, then that natural judgment and weight of character is cast aside, and that consistency which alone in deed and thought can keep up its own authority and what is seemly, can no longer be retained.

240. But fiercer passion springs from excessive anger, which the pain of some wrong received kindles within us. The monitions of the psalm which forms the opening of our subject instruct us on this point. Beautifully, then, has it come about that, in writing on duties, we used that declaration of our opening passage which also itself has to do with the direction of duty.

241. But since (as was but right) we there only touched upon the matter, as to how each one ought to take care not to be disturbed when wrong is done him, for fear that our preliminary remarks should run to too great length, I think that I will now discuss it a little more fully. For the occasion is opportune, as we are speaking on the different parts of temperance, to see how anger may be checked.

Chapter 48.

The argument for restraining anger is given again. Then the three classes of those who receive wrongs are set forth; to the most perfect of which the Apostle and David are said to have attained. He takes the opportunity to state the difference between this and the future life.

242. We wish if we can to point out three classes of men who receive wrongs in holy Scripture. One of these forms the class of those whom the sinner reviles, abuses, rides over rough-shod. And just because justice fails them, shame grows, pain increases. Very many of my own

order, of my own number, are like these. For if any one does me, who am weak, an injury, perhaps, though I am weak, I may forgive the wrong done me. If he charges me with an offense I am not such an one as to be content with the witness of my own conscience, although I know I am clear of what he brings against me; but I desire, just because I am weak, to wash out the mark of my inborn shame. Therefore I demand eye for eye, and tooth for tooth, and repay abuse with abuse.

243. If, however, I am one who is advancing, although not yet perfect, I do not return the reproaches; and if he breaks out into abuse, and fills my ears with reproaches, I am silent and do not answer.

244. But if I am perfect (I say this only by way of example, for in truth I am weak), if, then, I am perfect, I bless him that curses me, as Paul also blessed, for he says: Being reviled we bless. (1 Corinthians 4:12) He had heard Him Who says: Love your enemies, pray for them which despitefully use you and persecute you. (Matthew 5:44) And so Paul suffered persecution and endured it, for he conquered and calmed his human feelings for the sake of the reward set before him, namely, that he should become a son of God if he loved his enemies.

245. We call show, too, that holy David was like to Paul in this same class of virtue. When the son of Shimei cursed him, and charged him with heavy offenses, at the first he was silent and humbled himself, and was silent even about his good deeds, that is, his knowledge of good works. Then he even asked to be cursed; for when he was cursed he hoped to gain divine pity.

246. But see how he stored up humility and justice and prudence so as to merit grace from the Lord! At first he said: Therefore he cursed me, because the Lord has said unto him that he should curse. Here we have humility; for he thought that those things which are divinely ordered were to be endured with an even mind, as though he were but some servant lad. Then he said: Behold my son, which came forth of my bowels, seeks my life. Here we have justice. For if we suffer hard things at the hand of our own family, why are we angry at what is done to us by strangers? Lastly he says: Let him alone that he may curse, for the Lord has bidden him. It may be that the Lord will look on my humiliation and requite me good for this cursing. So he bore not only the abuse, but left the man unpunished when throwing stones and

following him. Nay, more, after his victory he freely granted him pardon when he asked for it.

247. I have written this to show that holy David, in true evangelical spirit, was not only not offended, but was even thankful to his abuser, and was delighted rather than angered by his wrongs, for which he thought some return would be granted to him. But, though perfect, he sought something still more perfect. As a man he grew hot at the pain of his wrongs, but like a good soldier he conquered, he endured like a brave wrestler. The end and aim of his patience was the expectation of the fulfilment of the promises, and therefore he said: Lord, make me to know mine end and the measure of my days, what it is: that I may know what is wanting to me. He seeks, then, that end of the heavenly promises, when each one shall arise in his own order: Christ the firstfruits, then they that are Christ's who have believed in His coming. Then comes the end. (1 Corinthians 15:23) For when the kingdom is delivered up to God, even the Father, and all the powers are put down, as the Apostle says, then perfection begins. Here, then, is the hindrance, here the weakness of the perfect; there full perfection. Thus it is he asks for those days of eternal life which are, and not for those which pass away, so that he may know what is wanting to him, what is the land of promise that bears everlasting fruits, which is the first mansion in his Father's house, which the second, which the third, wherein each one will rest according to his merits.

248. We then must strive for that wherein is perfection and wherein is truth. Here is the shadow, here the image; (Hebrews 10:1) there the truth. The shadow is in the law, the image in the Gospel, the truth in heaven. In old times a lamb, a Calf was offered; now Christ is offered. But He is offered as man and as enduring suffering. And He offers Himself as a priest to take away our sins, here in an image, there in truth, where with the Father He intercedes for us as our Advocate. Here, then, we walk in an image, we see in an image; there face to face where is full perfection. For all perfection rests in the truth.

Chapter 49.

We must reserve the likeness of the virtues in ourselves. The likeness of the devil and of vice must be got rid of, and especially that of avarice; for this deprives us of liberty, and despoils those who are in the midst of vanities of the image of God.

249. Whilst, then, we are here let us preserve the likeness, that there we may attain to the truth. Let the likeness of justice exist in us, likewise that of wisdom, for we shall come to that day and shall be rewarded according to our likeness.

250. Let not the adversary find his image in you, let him not find fury nor rage; for in these exists the likeness of wickedness. Our adversary the devil as a roaring lion seeks whom he may kill, whom he may devour. (1 Peter 5:8) Let him not find desire for gold, nor heaps of money, nor the appearance of vices, lest he take from you the voice of liberty. For the voice of true liberty is heard, when you can say: The prince of this world shall come, and shall find no part in me. (John 14:30) Therefore, if you are sure that he will find nothing in you, when he comes to search through you, you will say, as the patriarch Jacob did to Laban: Know now if there is anything of yours with me. (Genesis 31:32) Rightly do we account Jacob blessed with whom Laban could find naught of his. For Rachel had hidden the gold and silver images of his gods.

251. If, then, wisdom, and faith, and contempt of the world, and spiritual grace, exclude all faithlessness, you will be blessed; for you regard not vanity and folly and lying. Is it a light thing to take away from your adversary the opportunity to speak, so that he can have no ground to make his complaint against you? Thus he who looks not on vanity is not perturbed; but he who looks upon it is perturbed, and that, too, all to no purpose. Is it not a vain thing to heap up riches? For surely to seek for fleeting things is vain enough. And when you have gathered them, how do you know that you shall have them in possession?

252. Is it not vain for a merchant to journey by night and by day, that he may be able to heap up treasures? Is it not vain for him to gather merchandise, and to be much perturbed about its price, for fear he might sell it for less than he gave? That he should strive everywhere for high prices, and thus unexpectedly call up robbers against himself

through their envy at his much-vaunted business; or that, without waiting for calmer winds, impatient of delays, he should meet with shipwreck while seeking for gain?

253. And is not he, too, perturbed in vain who with great toil amasses wealth, though he knows not what heir to leave it to? Often and often all that an avaricious man has got together with the greatest care, his spendthrift heir scatters abroad with headlong prodigality. The shameless prodigal, blind to the present, heedless of the future, swallows up as in an abyss what took so long to gather. Often, too, the desired successor gains but envy for his share of the inheritance, and by his sudden death hands over the whole amount of the succession, which he has hardly entered upon, to strangers.

254. Why, then, do you idly spin a web which is worthless and fruitless? And why do you build up useless heaps of treasures like spiders' webs? For though they overflow, they are no good; nay, they denude you of the likeness of God, and put on you the likeness of the earthy. If any one has the likeness of the tyrant, is he not liable to condemnation? You lay aside the likeness of the Eternal King, and raisest in yourself the image of death. Rather cast out of the kingdom of your soul the likeness of the devil, and raise up the likeness of Christ. Let this shine forth in you; let this glow brightly in your kingdom, that is, your soul, for it destroys the likeness of all vices. David says of this: O Lord, in Your kingdom you bring their images to nothing. For when the Lord has adorned Jerusalem according to His own likeness, then every likeness of the adversary is destroyed.

Chapter 50.

The Levites ought to be utterly free from all earthly desires. What their virtues should be on the Apostle's own showing, and how great their purity must be. Also what their dignity and duty is, for the carrying out of which the chief virtues are necessary. He states that these were not unknown to the philosophers, but that they erred in their order. Some are by their nature in accordance with duty, which yet on account of what accompanies them become contrary to duty. From whence he gathers what gifts the office of the Levites demands. To conclude, he adds an exposition of Moses' words when blessing the tribe of Levi.

255. If, then, in the Gospel of the Lord the people themselves were taught and led to despise riches, (Mark 10:23) how much more ought ye Levites no longer to be bound down by earthly desires. For your portion is God. For when their earthly possessions were portioned out by Moses to the people of our fathers, the Lord suffered not the Levites to have a share in that earthly possession, (Numbers 18:23) for He Himself would be the strength of their inheritance. Wherefore David says: The Lord is the portion of mine inheritance and of my cup. Whence we get the name Levite, which means: Himself is mine, or Himself for me. Great, then, is his honour, that God should say of him: Himself is Mine. Or, as was said to Peter about the piece of money found in the fish's mouth: Give to them for Me and for you. (Matthew 17:27) Wherefore the Apostle, when he said: A bishop should be sober, modest, of good behaviour, given to hospitality, apt to teach, not covetous, nor a brawler, one that rules well his own house, also added: Likewise must the deacons be grave, not double-tongued, not given to much wine, not greedy of filthy lucre, holding the mystery of the faith in a pure conscience. And let them also first be proved, and so let them serve, being found blameless. (1 Timothy 3:2-10)

256. We note how much is required of us. The minister of the Lord should abstain from wine, so that he may be upheld by the good witness not only of the faithful but also by those who are without. For it is right that the witness to our acts and works should be the opinion of the public at large, that the office be not disgraced. Thus he who sees the minister of the altar adorned with suitable virtues may praise their Author, and reverence the Lord Who has such servants. The praise of the Lord sounds forth where there is a pure possession and an innocent rule at home.

Book One

257. But what shall I say about chastity, when only one and no second union is allowed? As regards marriage, the law is, not to marry again, nor to seek union with another wife. It seems strange to many why impediment should be caused by a second marriage entered on before baptism, so as to prevent election to the clerical office, and to the reception of the gift of ordination; seeing that even crimes are not wont to stand in the way, if they have been put away in the sacrament of baptism. But we must learn, that in baptism sin can be forgiven, but law cannot be abolished. In the case of marriage there is no sin, but there is a law. Whatever sin there is can be put away, whatever law there is cannot be laid aside in marriage. How could he exhort to widowhood who himself had married more than once?

258. But ye know that the ministerial office must be kept pure and unspotted, and must not be defiled by conjugal intercourse; ye know this, I say, who have received the gifts of the sacred ministry, with pure bodies, and unspoilt modesty, and without ever having enjoyed conjugal intercourse. I am mentioning this, because in some out-of-the-way places, when they enter on the ministry, or even when they become priests, they have begotten children. They defend this on the ground of old custom, when, as it happened, the sacrifice was offered up at long intervals. However, even the people had to be purified two or three days beforehand, so as to come clean to the sacrifice, as we read in the Old Testament. (Exodus 19:10) They even used to wash their clothes. If such regard was paid in what was only the figure, how much ought it to be shown in the reality! Learn then, Priest and Levite, what it means to wash your clothes. You must have a pure body wherewith to offer up the sacraments. If the people were forbidden to approach their victim unless they washed their clothes, do you, while foul in heart and body, dare to make supplication for others? Do you dare to make an offering for them?

259. The duty of the Levites is no light one, for the Lord says of them: Behold I have taken the Levites from among the children of Israel, instead of every first-born that opens the matrix among the children of Israel. These shall be their redemption, and the Levites shall be Mine. For I hallowed unto Me all the first-born in the land of Egypt. (Numbers 3:12-13) We know that the Levites are not reckoned among the rest, but are preferred before all, for they are chosen out of all, and are sanctified like the firstfruits and the firstlings which belong to the Lord, since the payment of vows and redemption for sin are offered by

them. You shall not receive them, He says, among the children of Israel, but you shall appoint the Levites over the tabernacle of testimony, and over all the vessels thereof, and over all things that belong to it. They shall bear the tabernacle and all the vessels thereof, and they shall minister in it, and shall encamp round about the tabernacle. And when the tabernacle sets forward the Levites shall take it down, and when the camp is pitched they shall set up the tabernacle again. And the stranger that comes near shall surely be put to death. (Numbers 1:49-51)

260. You, then, art chosen out of the whole number of the children of Israel, regarded as the firstfruits of the sacred offerings, set over the tabernacle so as to keep guard in the camp of holiness and faith, to which if a stranger approach, he shall surely die. You are placed there to watch over the ark of the covenant. All do not see the depths of the mysteries, for they are hid from the Levites, lest they should see who ought not to see, and they who cannot serve should take it up. Moses, indeed, saw the circumcision of the Spirit, but veiled it, so as to give circumcision only in an outward sign. He saw the unleavened bread of sincerity and truth; he saw the sufferings of the Lord, but he veiled the unleavened bread of truth in the material unleavened bread, he veiled the sufferings of the Lord in the sacrifice of a lamb or a calf. Good Levites have ever preserved the mystery entrusted to them under the protection of their own faith, and yet do you think little of what is entrusted to you? First, you shall see the deep things of God, which needs wisdom. Next, you must keep watch for the people; this requires justice. You must defend the camp and guard the tabernacle, which needs fortitude. You must show yourself continent and sober, and this needs temperance.

261. These chief virtues, they who are without have recognized, but they considered that the order resting on society was higher than that resting on wisdom; though wisdom is the foundation, and justice the building which cannot stand unless it have a foundation. The foundation is Christ. (1 Corinthians 3:11)

262. First stands faith, which is a sign of wisdom, as Solomon says, in following his father: The fear of the Lord is the beginning of wisdom. And the law says: You shall love the Lord your God, you shall love your neighbour. (Deuteronomy 6:5) It is a noble thing to do one's kindnesses and duties towards the whole of the human race. But it is ever most seemly that you should give to God the most precious thing you

have, that is, your mind, for you have nothing better than that. When you have paid your debt to your Creator, then you may labour for men, to show them kindness, and to give help; then you may assist the needy with money, or by some duty, or some service that lies in the way of your ministry; by money to support him; by paying a debt, so as to free him that is bound; by undertaking a duty, so as to take charge of a trust, which he fears to lose, who has put it by in trust.

263. It is a duty, then, to take care of and to restore what has been entrusted to us. But meanwhile a change comes, either in time or circumstances, so that it is no longer a duty to restore what one has received. As, for instance, when a man demands back his money as an open enemy, to use it against his country, and to offer his wealth to barbarians. Or, if you should have to restore it, while another stood by to extort it from him by force. If you restore money to a raving lunatic when he cannot keep it; if you give up to a madman a sword once put by with you, whereby he may kill himself, is it not an act contrary to duty to pay the debt? Is it not contrary to duty to take knowingly what has been got by a thief, so that he who has lost it is cheated out of it?

264. It is also sometimes contrary to duty to fulfil a promise, or to keep an oath. As was the case with Herod, who swore that whatever was asked he would give to the daughter of Herodias, and so allowed the death of John, that he might not break his word. And what shall I say of Jephthah, who offered up his daughter in sacrifice, she having been the first to meet him as he returned home victorious; whereby he fulfilled the vow which he had made that he would offer to God whatever should meet him first. It would have been better to make no promise at all, than to fulfil it in the death of his daughter.

265. You are not ignorant how important it is to look to this. And so a Levite is chosen to guard the sanctuary, one who shall never fail in counsel, nor forsake the faith, nor fear death, nor do anything extravagant, so that in his whole appearance he may give proof of his earnestness. For he ought to have not only his soul but even his eyes in restraint, so that no chance mishap may bring a blush to his forehead. For whosoever looks on a woman to desire her has already committed adultery with her in his heart. (Matthew 5:28) Thus adultery is committed not only by actual committal of the foul deed, but even by the desire of the ardent gaze.

266. This seems high and somewhat severe, but in a high office it is not out of place. For the grace of the Levites is such that Moses spoke of them as follows in his blessing: Give to Levi his men, give Levi his trusted ones, give Levi the lot of his inheritance, and his truth to the holy men whom they tempted in temptation, and reviled at the waters of contradiction. Who said to his father and mother, I know you not, and knew not his brethren, and renounced his children. He guarded Your word and kept Your testimony. (Deuteronomy 33:8-9)

267. They, then, are His men, His trusty ones, who have no deceit in their hearts, hide no treachery within them, but guard His words and ponder them in their heart, as Mary pondered them; (Luke 2:19) who know not their parents so as to put them before their duty; who hate the violators of chastity, and avenge the injury done to purity; and know the times for the fulfilling of their duty, as also which duty is the greater, which the lesser, and to what occasion each is suited. In all this they follow that alone which is virtuous. And who, where there are two virtuous duties, think that which is the more virtuous must come first. These are in truth rightly blessed.

268. If any one makes known the just works of the Lord, and offers Him incense, then: Bless, O Lord, his strength; accept the work of his hands, (Deuteronomy 33:11) that he may find the grace of the prophetic blessing with Him Who lives and reigns for ever and ever. Amen.

BOOK TWO

Chapter 1.

Happiness in life is to be gained by living virtuously, inasmuch as thus a Christian, whilst despising glory and the favour of men, desires to please God alone in what he does.

1. In the first book we spoke of the duties which we thought befitted a virtuous life, whereon no one has ever doubted but that a blessed life, which the Scripture calls eternal life, depends. So great is the splendour of a virtuous life that a peaceful conscience and a calm innocence work out a happy life. And as the risen sun hides the globe of the moon and the light of the stars, so the brightness of a virtuous life, where it glitters in true pure glory, casts into the shade all other things, which, according to the desires of the body, are considered to be good, or are reckoned in the eyes of the world to be great and noble.

2. Blessed, plainly, is that life which is not valued at the estimation of outsiders, but is known, as judge of itself, by its own inner feelings. It needs no popular opinion as its reward in any way; nor has it any fear of punishments. Thus the less it strives for glory, the more it rises above it. For to those who seek for glory, that reward in the shape of present things is but a shadow of future ones, and is a hindrance to eternal life, as it is written in the Scriptures: Verily, I say unto you, they have received their reward. (Matthew 6:2) This is said of those who, as it were, with the sound of a trumpet desire to make known to all the world the liberality they exercise towards the poor. It is the same, too, in the case of fasting, which is done but for outward show. They have, he says, their reward.

3. It therefore belongs to a virtuous life to show mercy and to fast in secret; that you may seem to be seeking a reward from your God alone, and not from men. For he who seeks it from man has his reward, but he who seeks it from God has eternal life, which none can give but the Lord of Eternity, as it is said: Verily, I say unto you, today shall you be with Me in Paradise. (Luke 23:43) Wherefore the Scripture plainly has called that life which is blessed, eternal life. It has not been left to be appraised according to man's ideas on the subject, but has been entrusted to the divine judgment.

Chapter 2.

The different ideas of philosophers on the subject of happiness. He proves, first, from the Gospel that it rests on the knowledge of God and the pursuit of good works; next, that it may not be thought that this idea was adopted from the philosophers, he adds proofs from the witness of the prophets.

4. The philosophers have made a happy life to depend, either (as Hieronymus) on freedom from pain, or (as Herillus) on knowledge. For Herillus, hearing knowledge very highly praised by Aristotle and Theophrastus, made it alone to be the chief good, when they really praised it as a good thing, not as the only good; others, as Epicurus, have called pleasure such; others, as Callipho, and after him Diodorus, understood it in such a way as to make a virtuous life go in union, the one with pleasure, the other with freedom from pain, since a happy life could not exist without it. Zeno, the Stoic, thought the highest and only good existed in a virtuous life. But Aristotle and Theophrastus and the other Peripatetics maintained that a happy life consisted in virtue, that is, in a virtuous life, but that its happiness was made complete by the advantages of the body and other external good things.

5. But the sacred Scriptures say that eternal life rests on a knowledge of divine things and on the fruit of good works. The Gospel bears witness to both these statements. For the Lord Jesus spoke thus of knowledge: This is eternal life, to know You, the only true God, and Jesus Christ Whom You have sent. (John 17:3) About works He gives this answer: Every one that has forsaken house, or brethren, or sisters, or father, or mother, or wife, or children, or lands, for My Name's sake, shall receive an hundred-fold, and shall inherit everlasting life. (Matthew 19:29)

6. Let no one think that this was but lately said, and that it was spoken of by the philosophers before it was mentioned in the Gospel. For the philosophers, that is to say, Aristotle and Theophrastus, as also Zeno and Hieronymus, certainly lived before the time of the Gospel; but they came after the prophets. Let them rather think how long before even the names of the philosophers were heard of, both of these seem to have found open expression through the mouth of the holy David; for it is written: Blessed is the man whom You instruct, O Lord, and teach him out of Your law. We find elsewhere also: Blessed is the man that fears the Lord, he will rejoice greatly in His commandments. We have proved our point as regards knowledge, the reward for which the prophet states to be the fruit of eternity, adding that in the house of the man that fears the Lord, or is instructed in His law and rejoices greatly in the divine commandments, is glory and riches; and his justice abides for ever and ever. He has further also in the same psalm stated of good works, that they gain for an upright man the gift of eternal life. He speaks thus: Blessed is the man that shows pity and lends, he will guide his affairs with discretion, surely he shall not be moved for ever, the righteous shall be in everlasting remembrance. And further: He has dispersed, he has given to the poor, his justice endures for ever.

7. Faith, then, has [the promise of] eternal life, for it is a good foundation. Good works, too, have the same, for an upright man is tested by his words and acts. For if a man is always busy talking and yet is slow to act, he shows by his acts how worthless his knowledge is: besides it is much worse to know what one ought to do, and yet not to do what one has learned should be done. On the other hand, to be active in good works and unfaithful at heart is as idle as though one wanted to raise a beautiful and lofty dome upon a bad foundation. The higher one builds, the greater is the fall; for without the protection of faith good works cannot stand. A treacherous anchorage in a harbour perforates a ship, and a sandy bottom quickly gives way and cannot bear the weight of the building placed upon it. There then will be found the fullness of reward, where the virtues are perfect, and where there is a reasonable agreement between words and acts.

Chapter 3.

The definition of blessedness as drawn from the Scriptures is considered and proved. It cannot be enhanced by external good fortune, nor can it be weakened by misfortune.

8. As, then, knowledge, so far as it stands alone, is put aside either as worthless, according to the superfluous discussions of the philosophers, or as but an imperfect idea, let us now note how clearly the divine Scriptures explain a thing about which we see the philosophers held so many involved and perplexing ideas. For the Scriptures state that nothing is good but what is virtuous, and declare that virtue is blessed in every circumstance, and that it is never enhanced by either corporal or other external good fortune, nor is it weakened by adversity. No state is so blessed as that wherein one is free from sin, is filled with innocence, and is fully supplied with the grace of God. For it is written: Blessed is the man that has not walked in the counsel of the ungodly, and has not stood in the way of sinners, and has not sat in the seat of pestilence, but in the law of the Lord was his delight. And again: Blessed are the undefiled in the way, who walk in the law of the Lord.

9. Innocence, then, and knowledge make a man blessed. We have also noted already that the blessedness of eternal life is the reward for good works. It remains, then, to show that when the patronage of pleasure or the fear of pain is despised (and the first of these one abhors as poor and effeminate, and the other as unmanly and weak), that then a blessed life can rise up in the midst of pain. This can easily be shown when we read: Blessed are you when men shall revile you and persecute you and shall say all manner of evil against you for righteousness' sake. Rejoice and be exceeding glad, for great is your reward in heaven; for so persecuted they the prophets which were before you. (Matthew 5:11-12) And again: He that will come after Me, let him take up his cross and follow Me. (Matthew 16:24)

Book Two

Chapter 4.

The same argument, namely, that blessedness is not lessened or added to by external matters, is illustrated by the example of men of old.

10. There is, then, a blessedness even in pains and griefs. All which virtue with its sweetness checks and restrains, abounding as it does in natural resources for either soothing conscience or increasing grace. For Moses was blessed in no small degree when, surrounded by the Egyptians and shut in by the sea, he found by his merits a way for himself and the people to go through the waters. Exodus xiv When was he ever braver than at the moment when, surrounded by the greatest dangers, he gave not up the hope of safety, but besought a triumph?

11. What of Aaron? When did he ever think himself more blessed than when he stood between the living and the dead, and by his presence stayed death from passing from the bodies of the dead to the lines of the living? (Numbers 16:48) What shall I say of the youth Daniel, who was so wise that, when in the midst of the lions enraged with hunger, he was by no means overcome with terror at the fierceness of the beasts. So free from fear was he, that he could eat, and was not afraid he might by his example excite the animals to feed on him.

12. There is, then, in pain a virtue that can display the sweetness of a good conscience, and therefore it serves as a proof that pain does not lessen the pleasure of virtue. As, then, there is no loss of blessedness to virtue through pain, so also the pleasures of the body and the enjoyment that benefits give add nothing to it. On this the Apostle says well: What things to me were gain, those I counted loss for Christ, and he added: Wherefore I count all things but loss, and do count them but dung, that I may win Christ. (Philippians 3:7-8)

13. Moses, too, thought the treasures of Egypt to be his loss, and thus showed forth in his life the reproach of the Cross of the Lord. He was not rich when he had abundance of money, nor was he afterwards poor when he was in want of food, unless, perchance, there is any one who thinks he was less happy when daily food was wanting to him and his people in the wilderness. But yet manna, that is, angels' food, which surely none will dare deny to be a mark of the greatest good and of blessedness, was given him from heaven; also the daily shower of meat was sufficient to feed the whole multitude. (Exodus 16:13)

14. Bread for food also failed Elijah, that holy man, had he sought for it; but it seemed not to fail him because he sought it not. Thus by the daily service of the ravens bread was brought to him in the morning, meat in the evening. Was he any the less blessed because he was poor to himself? Certainly not. Nay, he was the more blessed, for he was rich toward God. It is better to be rich for others than for oneself. He was so, for in the time of famine he asked a widow for food, intending to repay it, so that the barrel of meal failed not for three years and six months, and the oil jar sufficed and served the needy widow for her daily use all that time also. Rightly did Peter wish to be there where he saw them. Rightly did they appear in the mount with Christ in glory, (Matthew 17:3) for He Himself became poor when He was rich.

15. Riches, then, give no assistance to living a blessed life, a fact that the Lord clearly shows in the Gospel, saying: Blessed are you poor, for yours is the kingdom of God. Blessed are they that hunger and thirst now, for they shall be filled. Blessed are you that weep now, for you shall laugh. (Luke 6:20-21) Thus it is stated as plainly as possible that poverty, hunger, and pain, which are considered to be evils, not only are not hindrances to a blessed life, but are actually so many helps toward it.

Chapter 5.

Those things which are generally looked on as good are mostly hindrances to a blessed life, and those which are looked on as evil are the materials out of which virtues grow. What belongs to blessedness is shown by other examples.

16. But those things which seem to be good, as riches, abundance, joy without pain, are a hindrance to the fruits of blessedness, as is clearly stated in the Lord's own words, when He said: Woe to you rich, for you have received your consolation! Woe unto you that are full, for you shall hunger, and to those who laugh, for they shall mourn! (Luke 6:24-25) So, then, corporal or external good things are not only no assistance to attaining a blessed life, but are even a hindrance to it.

17. Wherefore Naboth was blessed, even though he was stoned by the rich; weak and poor, as opposed to the royal resources, he was rich in his aim and his religion; so rich, indeed, that he would not exchange the inheritance of the vineyard received from his father for the king's

money; and on this account was he perfect, for he defended the rights of his forefathers with his own blood. Thus, also, Ahab was wretched on his own showing, for he caused the poor man to be put to death, so as to take possession of his vineyard himself.

18. It is quite certain that virtue is the only and the highest good; that it alone richly abounds in the fruit of a blessed life; that a blessed life, by means of which eternal life is won, does not depend on external or corporal benefits, but on virtue only. A blessed life is the fruit of the present, and eternal life is the hope of the future.

19. Some, however, there are who think a blessed life is impossible in this body, weak and fragile as it is. For in it one must suffer pain and grief, one must weep, one must be ill. So I could also say that a blessed life rests on bodily rejoicing, but not on the heights of wisdom, on the sweetness of conscience, or on the loftiness of virtue. It is not a blessed thing to be in the midst of suffering; but it is blessed to be victorious over it, and not to be cowed by the power of temporal pain.

20. Suppose that things come which are accounted terrible as regards the grief they cause, such as blindness, exile, hunger, violation of a daughter, loss of children. Who will deny that Isaac was blessed, who did not see in his old age, and yet gave blessings with his benediction? (Genesis 27:28) Was not Jacob blessed who, leaving his father's house, endured exile as a shepherd for pay, (Genesis 31:41) and mourned for the violated chastity of his daughter, (Genesis 34:5) and suffered hunger? (Genesis 42:2) Were they not blessed on whose good faith God received witness, as it is written: The God of Abraham, the God of Isaac, and the God of Jacob? (Exodus 3:6) A wretched thing is slavery, but Joseph was not wretched; nay, clearly he was blessed, when he while in slavery checked the lusts of his mistress. (Genesis 39:7) What shall I say of holy David who bewailed the death of three sons, and, what was even worse than this, his daughter's incestuous connection? How could he be unblessed from whom the Author of blessedness Himself sprung, Who has made many blessed? For: Blessed are they who have not seen yet have believed. (John 20:29) All these felt their own weakness, but they bravely prevailed over it. What can we think of as more wretched than holy Job, either in the burning of his house, or the instantaneous death of his ten sons, or his bodily pains? Was he less blessed than if he had not endured those things whereby he really showed himself approved?

21. True it is that in these sufferings there is something bitter, and that strength of mind cannot hide this pain. I should not deny that the sea is deep because inshore it is shallow, nor that the sky is clear because sometimes it is covered with clouds, nor that the earth is fruitful because in some places there is but barren ground, nor that the crops are rich and full because they sometimes have wild oats mingled with them. So, too, count it as true that the harvest of a happy conscience may be mingled with some bitter feelings of grief. In the sheaves of the whole of a blessed life, if by chance any misfortune or bitterness has crept in, is it not as though the wild oats were hidden, or as though the bitterness of the tares was concealed by the sweet scent of the grain? But let us now proceed again with our subject.

Chapter 6.

On what is useful: not that which is advantageous, but that which is just and virtuous. It is to be found in losses, and is divided into what is useful for the body, and what is useful unto godliness.

22. In the first book we made our division in such a way as to set in the first place what is virtuous and what is seemly; for all duties are derived from these. In the second place we set what is useful. But as at the start we said that there was a difference between what is virtuous and what is seemly— which one can comprehend more easily than one can explain— so also when we are thinking of what is useful, we have to give considerable thought to what is the more useful.

23. But we do not reckon usefulness by the value of any gain in money, but in acquiring godliness, as the Apostle says: But godliness is profitable unto all things, having promise of the life that now is, and of that which is to come. (1 Timothy 4:8) Thus in the holy Scriptures, if we look carefully we shall often find that what is virtuous is called useful: All things are lawful unto me, but all things are not profitable [useful]. (1 Corinthians 6:12) Before that he was speaking of vices, and so means: It is lawful to sin, but it is not seemly. Sins rest in one's own power, but they are not virtuous. To live wantonly is easy, but it is not right. For food serves not God but the belly.

24. Therefore, because what is useful is also just, it is just to serve Christ, Who redeemed us. They too are just who for His Name's sake have given themselves up to death, they are unjust who have avoided

Book Two

it. Of them it says: What profit is there in my blood? that is: what advance has my justice made? Wherefore they also say: Let us bind the just, for he is useless to us, that is: he is unjust, for he complains of us, condemns and rebukes us. This could also be referred to the greed of impious men, which closely resembles treachery; as we read in the case of the traitor Judas, who in his longing for gain and his desire for money put his head into the noose of treachery and fell.

25. We have then to speak of that usefulness which is full of what is virtuous, as the Apostle himself has laid it down in so many words, saying: And this I speak for your own profit, not that I may cast a snare upon you, but for that which is comely. (1 Corinthians 7:35) It is plain, then, that what is virtuous is useful, and what is useful is virtuous; also that what is useful is just, and what is just is useful. I can say this, for I am speaking, not to merchants who are covetous from a desire to make gain, but to my children. And I am speaking of the duties which I wish to impress upon and impart to you, whom I have chosen for the service of the Lord; so that those things which have been already implanted and fixed in your minds and characters by habit and training may now be further unfolded to you by explanation and instruction.

26. Therefore as I am about to speak of what is useful, I will take up those words of the Prophet: Incline my heart unto Your testimonies and not to covetousness, that the sound of the word useful may not rouse in us the desire for money. Some indeed put it thus: Incline my heart unto Your testimonies and not to what is useful, that is, that kind of usefulness which is always on the watch for making gains in business, and has been bent and diverted by the habits of men to the pursuit of money. For as a rule most people call that only useful which is profitable, but we are speaking of that kind of usefulness which is sought in earthly loss that we may gain Christ, (Philippians 3:8) whose gain is godliness with contentment. (1 Timothy 6:6) Great, too, is the gain whereby we attain to godliness, which is rich with God, not indeed in fleeting wealth, but in eternal gifts, and in which rests no uncertain trial but grace constant and unending.

27. There is therefore a usefulness connected with the body, and also one that has to do with godliness, according to the Apostle's division: Bodily exercise profits a little, but godliness is profitable unto all things. (1 Timothy 4:8) And what is so virtuous as integrity? What so

seemly as to preserve the body unspotted and undefiled, and its purity unsullied? What, again, is so seemly as that a widow should keep her plighted troth to her dead husband? What more useful than this whereby the heavenly kingdom is attained? For there are some who have made themselves eunuchs for the kingdom of heaven's sake. (Matthew 19:12)

Chapter 7.

What is useful is the same as what is virtuous; nothing is more useful than love, which is gained by gentleness, courtesy, kindness, justice, and the other virtues, as we are given to understand from the histories of Moses and David. Lastly, confidence springs from love, and again love from confidence.

28. There is therefore not only a close intercourse between what is virtuous and what is useful, but the same thing is both useful and virtuous. Therefore He Who willed to open the kingdom of heaven to all sought not what was useful to Himself, but what was useful for all. Thus we must have a certain order and proceed step by step from habitual or common acts to those which are more excellent, so as to show by many examples the advancement of what is useful.

29. And first we may know there is nothing so useful as to be loved, nothing so useless as not to be loved; for to be hated in my opinion is simply fatal and altogether deadly. We speak of this, then, in order that we may take care to give cause for a good estimate and opinion to be formed of us, and may try to get a place in others' affections through our calmness of mind and kindness of soul. For goodness is agreeable and pleasing to all, and there is nothing that so easily reaches human feelings. And if that is assisted by gentleness of character and willingness, as well as by moderation in giving orders and courtesy of speech, by honour in word, by a ready interchange of conversation and by the grace of modesty, it is incredible how much all this tends to an increase of love.

30. We read, not only in the case of private individuals but even of kings, what is the effect of ready and willing courtesy, and what harm pride and great swelling words have done, so far as to make even kingdoms to totter and powers to be destroyed. If any one gains the people's favour by advice or service, by fulfilling the duties of his min-

istry or office, or if he encounters danger for the sake of the whole nation, there is no doubt but that such love will be shown him by the people that they all will put his safety and welfare before their own.

31. What reproaches Moses had to bear from his people! But when the Lord would have avenged him on those who reviled him, he often used to offer himself for the people that he might save them from the divine anger. (Exodus 32:32) With what gentle words used he to address the people, even after he was wronged! He comforted them in their labours, consoled them by his prophetic declarations of the future, and encouraged them by his works. And though he often spoke with God, yet he was wont to address men gently and pleasantly. Worthily was he considered to stand above all men. For they could not even look on his face, (Exodus 34:30) and refused to believe that his sepulchre was found. (Deuteronomy 34:6) He had captivated the minds of all the people to such an extent; that they loved him even more for his gentleness than they admired him for his deeds.

32. There is David too who followed his steps, who was chosen from among all to rule the people. How gentle and kindly he was, humble in spirit too, how diligent and ready to show affection. Before he came to the throne he offered himself in the stead of all. As king he showed himself an equal to all in warfare, and shared in their labours. He was brave in battle, gentle in ruling, patient under abuse, and more ready to bear than to return wrongs. So dear was he to all, that though a youth, he was chosen even against his will to rule over them, and was made to undertake the duty though he withstood it. When old he was asked by his people not to engage in battle, because they all preferred to incur danger for his sake rather than that he should undergo it for theirs.

33. He had bound the people to himself freely in doing his duty; first, when he during the division among the people preferred to live like an exile at Hebron rather than to reign at Jerusalem; next, when he showed that he loved valour even in an enemy. He had also thought that justice should be shown to those who had borne arms against himself the same as to his own men. Again, he admired Abner, the bravest champion of the opposing side, while he was their leader and was yet waging war. Nor did he despise him when suing for peace, but honoured him by a banquet. When killed by treachery, he mourned and wept for him. He followed him and honoured his obsequies, and evinced his good faith in desiring vengeance for the murder; for he

handed on that duty to his son in the charge that he gave him, being anxious rather that the death of an innocent man should not be left unavenged, than that any one should mourn for his own.

34. It is no small thing, especially in the case of a king, so to perform humble duties as to make oneself like the very lowest. It is noble not to seek for food at another's risk and to refuse a drink of water, to confess a sin, and to offer oneself to death for one's people. This latter David did, so that the divine anger might be turned against himself, when he offered himself to the destroying angel and said: Lo I have sinned: I the shepherd have done wickedly, but this flock, what has it done? Let Your hand be against me.

35. What further should I say? He opened not his mouth to those planning deceit, and, as though hearing not, he thought no word should be returned, nor did be answer their reproaches. When he was evil spoken of, he prayed, when he was cursed, he blessed. He walked in simplicity of heart, and fled from the proud. He was a follower of those unspotted from the world, one who mixed ashes with his food when bewailing his sins, and mingled his drink with weeping. Worthily, then, was he called for by all the people. All the tribes of Israel came to him saying: Behold, we are your bone and your flesh. Also yesterday and the day before when Saul lived, and reigned, you were he that leddest out and brought in Israel. And the Lord said to you, You shall feed My people! And why should I say more about him of whom the word of the Lord has gone forth to say: I have found David according to My heart? Who ever walked in holiness of heart and in justice as he did, so as to fulfil the will of God; for whose sake pardon was granted to his children when they sinned, and their rights were preserved to his heirs?

36. Who would not have loved him, when they saw how dear he was to his friends? For as he truly loved his friends, so he thought that he was loved as much in return by his own friends. Nay, parents put him even before their own children, and children loved him more than their parents. Wherefore Saul was very angry and strove to strike Jonathan his son with a spear because he thought that David's friendship held a higher place in his esteem than either filial piety or a father's authority.

37. It gives a very great impetus to mutual love if one shows love in return to those who love us and proves that one does not love them

Book Two

less than oneself is loved, especially if one shows it by the proofs that a faithful friendship gives. What is so likely to win favour as gratitude? What more natural than to love one who loves us? What so implanted and so impressed on men's feelings as the wish to let another, by whom we want to be loved, know that we love him? Well does the wise man say: Lose your money for your brother and your friend. (Sirach 29:10) And again: I will not be ashamed to defend a friend, neither will I hide myself from him. (Sirach 22:31) If, indeed, the words in Ecclesiasticus testify that the medicine of life and immortality is in a friend; (Sirach 6:16) yet none has ever doubted that it is in love that our best defence lies. As the Apostle says: It bears all things, believes all things, hopes all things, endures all things; love never fails. (1 Corinthians 13:7-8)

38. Thus David failed not, for he was dear to all, and wished to be loved rather than feared by his subjects. Fear keeps the watch of temporal protection, but knows not how to keep guard permanently. And so where fear has departed, boldness often creeps in; for fear does not force confidence but affection calls it forth.

39. Love, then, is the first thing to give us a recommendation. It is a good thing therefore to have our witness in the love of many. Then arises confidence, so that even strangers are not afraid to trust themselves to your kindness, when they see you so dear to many. So likewise one goes through confidence to love, so that he who has shown good faith to one or two has an influence as it were on the minds of all, and wins the good-will of all.

Chapter 8.

Nothing has greater effect in gaining good-will than giving advice; but none can trust it unless it rests on justice and prudence. How conspicuous these two virtues were in Solomon is shown by his well-known judgment.

40. Two things, therefore, love and confidence, are the most efficacious in commending us to others; also this third quality if you have it, namely, what many consider to be worthy of admiration in you, and think to be rightly worthy of honour [the power, in fact, of giving good advice].

41. Since the giving of good advice is a great means of gaining men's affections, prudence and justice are much needed in every case. These are looked for by most, so that confidence at once is placed in him in whom they exist, because he can give useful and trustworthy advice to whoever wants it. Who will put himself into the hands of a man whom he does not think to be more wise than himself who asks for advice? It is necessary therefore that he of whom advice is asked should be superior to him who asks it. For why should we consult a man when we do not think that he can make anything more plain than we ourselves see it?

42. But if we have found a man that by the vigour of his character, by his strength of mind and influence, stands forth above all others, and further, is better fitted by example and experience than others; that can put an end to immediate dangers, foresee future ones, point out those close at hand, can explain a subject, bring relief in time, is ready not only to give advice but also to give help—in such a man confidence is placed, so that he who seeks advice can say: Though evil should happen to me through him, I will bear it. (Sirach 22:31)

43. To a man of this sort then we entrust our safety and our reputation, for he is, as we said before, just and prudent. Justice causes us to have no fear of deceit, and prudence frees us from having any suspicions of error. However, we trust ourselves more readily to a just than to a prudent man, to put it in the way people generally do. But, according to the definition of the philosophers, where there is one virtue, others exist too, while prudence cannot exist without justice. We find this stated also in our writers, for David says: The just shows mercy and lends. What the just lends, he says elsewhere: A good man is he that shows mercy and lends, he will guide his words with discretion.

44. Is not that noble judgment of Solomon full of wisdom and justice? Let us see whether it is so. Two women, it says, stood before King Solomon, and the one said to him, Hear me, my lord, I and this woman dwell in one house, and before the third day we gave birth and bore a son apiece, and were together, there was no witness in the house, nor any other woman with us, only we two alone. And her son died this night, because she overlaid it, and she arose at midnight, and took my son from my breast, and laid it in her bosom, and her dead child she laid at my breast. And I arose in the morning to give my child suck, and found him dead. And I considered it at dawn, and behold it was

not my son. And the other woman said, Nay, but the living is my son, and the dead is your son.

45. This was their dispute, in which either tried to claim the living child for herself, and denied that the dead one was hers. Then the king commanded a sword to be brought and the infant to be cut in half, and either piece to be given to one, one half to the one, and one half to the other. Then the woman whose the child really was, moved by her feelings, cried out: Divide not the child, my lord; let it rather be given to her and live, and do not kill it. But the other answered: Let it be neither mine nor hers, divide it. Then the king ordered that the infant should be given to the woman who had said: Do not kill it, but give it to that woman; For, as it says, her bowels yearned upon her son.

46. It is not wrong to suppose that the mind of God was in him; for what is hidden from God? What can be more hidden than the witness that lies deep within; into which the mind of the wise king entered as though to judge a mother's feelings, and elicited as it were the voice of a mother's heart. For a mother's feelings were laid bare, when she chose that her son should live with another, rather than that he should be killed in his mother's sight.

47. It was therefore a sign of wisdom to distinguish between secret heart-thoughts, to draw the truth from hidden springs, and to pierce as it were with the sword of the Spirit not only the inward parts of the body, but even of the mind and soul. It was the part of justice also that she who had killed her own child should not take away another's, but that the real mother should have her own back again. Indeed the Scriptures have declared this. All Israel, it says, heard of the judgment which the king had judged, and they feared the king, for they saw that the wisdom of God was in him to do judgment. Solomon also himself had asked for wisdom, so that a prudent heart might be given him to hear and to judge with justice.

Chapter 9.

Though justice and prudence are inseparable, we must have respect to the ideas of people in general, for they make a distinction between the different cardinal virtues.

48. It is clear also, according to the sacred Scriptures, which are the older, that wisdom cannot exist without justice, for where one of these two is, the other must be also. With what wisdom did Daniel expose the lie in the false accusation brought against him by his thorough examination, so that those false informers had no answer ready to hand! It was a mark of prudence to convict the criminals by the witness of their own words, and a sign of justice to give over the guilty to punishment, and to save the innocent from it.

49. There is therefore an inseparable union between wisdom and justice; but, generally speaking, the one special form of virtue is divided up. Thus temperance lies in despising pleasures, fortitude may be seen in undergoing labours and dangers, prudence in the choice of what is good, by knowing how to distinguish between things useful and the reverse; justice, in being a good guardian of another's rights and protector of its own, thus maintaining for each his own. We can make this fourfold division in deference to commonly received ideas; and so, while deviating from those subtle discussions of philosophic learning which are brought forth as though from some inner recess for the sake of investigating the truth, can follow the commonly received use and their ordinary meaning. Keeping, then, to this division, let us return to our subject.

Chapter 10.

Men entrust their safety rather to a just than to a prudent man. But every one is wont to seek out the man who combines in himself the qualities of justice and prudence. Solomon gives us an example of this. (The words which the queen of Sheba spoke of him are explained.) Also Daniel and Joseph.

50. We entrust our case to the most prudent man we can find, and ask advice from him more readily than we do from others. However, the faithful counsel of a just man stands first and often has more weight than the great abilities of the wisest of men: For better are the wounds

Book Two

of a friend than the kisses of others. (Proverbs 27:6) And just because it is the judgment of a just man, it is also the conclusion of a wise one: in the one lies the result of the matter in dispute, in the other readiness of invention.

51. And if one connects the two, there will be great soundness in the advice given, which is regarded by all with admiration for the wisdom shown, and with love for its justice. And so all will desire to hear the wisdom of that man in whom those two virtues are found together, as all the kings of the earth desired to see the face of Solomon and to hear his wisdom. Nay, even the queen of Sheba came to him and tried him with questions. She came and spoke of all the things that were in her heart, and heard all the wisdom of Solomon, nor did any word escape her.

52. Who she was whom nothing escaped, and that there was nothing which the truth-loving Solomon did not tell her, learn, O man, from this which you hear her saying: It was a true report that I heard in my own land of your words and of your prudence, yet I did not believe those that told it me until I came, and my eyes had seen it; and behold the half was not told me. You have added good things over and above all that I heard in my own land. Blessed are your women and blessed your servants, which stand before you, and that hear all your prudence. Recognize the feast of the true Solomon, and who are set down at that feast; recognize it wisely and think in what land all the nations shall hear the fame of true wisdom and justice, and with what eyes they shall see Him, beholding those things which are not seen. For the things that are seen are temporal, but the things which are not seen are eternal. (2 Corinthians 4:18)

53. What women are blessed but those of whom it is said that many hear the word of God and bring forth fruit? (Luke 11:28) And again: Whosoever does the word of God is My father and sister and mother. (Matthew 12:50) And who are those blessed servants, who stand before Him, but Paul, who said: Even to this day I stand witnessing both to great and small; (Acts 26:22) or Simeon, who was waiting in the temple to see the consolation of Israel? (Luke 2:25) How could he have asked to be let depart, except that in standing before the Lord he had not the power of departing, but only according to the will of God? Solomon is put before us simply for the sake of example, of whom it was eagerly expected that his wisdom should be heard.

54. Joseph also when in prison was not free from being consulted about matters of uncertainty. His counsel was of advantage to the whole of Egypt, so that it felt not the seven years' famine, and he was able even to relieve other peoples from their dreadful hunger.

55. Daniel, though one of the captives, was made the head of the royal counsellors. By his counsels he improved the present and foretold the future. Daniel ii Confidence was put in him in all things, because he had frequently interpreted things, and had shown that he had declared the truth.

Chapter 11.

A third element which tends to gain any one's confidence is shown to have been conspicuous in Moses, Daniel, and Joseph.

56. But a third point seems also to have been noted in the case of those who were thought worthy of admiration after the example of Joseph, Solomon, and Daniel. For what shall I say of Moses whose advice all Israel always waited for, (Exodus 18:13) whose life caused them to trust in his prudence and increased their esteem for him? Who would not trust to the counsel of Moses, to whom the elders reserved for decision whatever they thought beyond their understanding and powers?

57. Who would refuse the counsel of Daniel, of whom God Himself said: Who is wiser than Daniel? (Ezekiel 28:3) How can men doubt about the minds of those to whom God has given such grace? By the counsel of Moses wars were brought to an end, and for his merit's sake food came from heaven and drink from the rock.

58. How pure must have been the soul of Daniel to soften the character of barbarians and to tame the lions! What temperance was his, what self-restraint in soul and body! Not unworthily did he become an object of admiration to all, when— and all men do admire this—though enjoying royal friendships, he sought not for gold, nor counted the honour given him as more precious than his faith. For he was willing to endure danger for the law of God rather than to be turned from his purpose in order to gain the favour of men.

59. And what, again, shall I say of the chastity and justice of Joseph, whom I had almost passed by, whereby on the one hand he rejected

the allurements of his mistress and refused rewards, on the other he mocked at death, repressed his fear, and chose a prison? Who would not consider him a fit person to give advice in a private case, whose fruitful spirit and fertile mind enriched the barrenness of the time with the wealth of his counsels and heart?

Chapter 12.

No one asks counsel from a man tainted with vice, or from one who is morose or impracticable, but rather from one of whom we have a pattern in the Scriptures.

60. We note therefore that in seeking for counsel, uprightness of life, excellence in virtues, habits of benevolence, and the charm of good-nature have very great weight. Who seeks for a spring in the mud? Who wants to drink from muddy water? So where there is luxurious living, excess, and a union of vices, who will think that he ought to draw from that source? Who does not despise a foul life? Who will think a man to be useful to another's cause whom he sees to be useless in his own life? Who, again, does not avoid a wicked, ill-disposed, abusive person, who is always ready to do harm? Who would not be only too eager to avoid him?

61. And who will come to a man however well fitted to give the best of advice who is nevertheless hard to approach? It goes with him as with a fountain whose waters are shut off. What is the advantage of having wisdom, if one refuses to give advice? If one cuts off the opportunities of giving advice, the source is closed, so as no longer to flow for others or to be of any good to oneself.

62. Well can we refer this to him who, possessing prudence, has defiled it with the foulness of a vicious life and so pollutes the water at the source. His life is a proof of a degenerate spirit. How can one judge him to be good in counsel whom one sees to be evil in character? He ought to be superior to me, if I am ready to trust myself to him. Am I to suppose that he is fit to give me advice who never takes it for himself, or am I to believe that he has time to give to me when he has none for himself, when his mind is filled with pleasures, and he is overcome by lust, is the slave of avarice, is excited by greed, and is terrified with fright? How is there room for counsel here where there is none for quiet?

63. That man of counsel whom I must admire and look up to, whom the gracious Lord gave to our fathers, put aside all that was offensive. His follower he ought to be, who can give counsel and protect another's prudence from vice; for nothing foul can mingle with that.

Chapter 13.

The beauty of wisdom is made plain by the divine testimony. From this he goes on to prove its connection with the other virtues.

64. Is there any one who would like to be beautiful in face and at the same time to have its charm spoilt by a beast-like body and fearful talons? Now the form of virtues is so wonderful and glorious, and especially the beauty of wisdom, as the whole of the Scriptures tell us. For it is more brilliant than the sun, and when compared with the stars far outshines any constellation. Night takes their light away in its train, but wickedness cannot overcome wisdom. (Wisdom 7:29-30)

65. We have spoken of its beauty, and proved it by the witness of Scripture. It remains to show on the authority of Scripture (Wisdom 7:22-23) that there can be no fellowship between it and vice, but that it has an inseparable union with the rest of the virtues. It has a spirit sagacious, undefiled, sure, holy, loving what is good, quick, that never forbids a kindness, kind, steadfast, free from care, having all power, overseeing all things. And again: (Wisdom 8:7) She teaches temperance and justice and virtue.

Chapter 14.

Prudence is combined with all the virtues, especially with contempt of riches.

66. Prudence, therefore, works through all things, she has fellowship with all that is good. For how can she give good advice unless she have justice too, so that she may clothe herself in consistency, not fear death, be held back by no alarm, no fear, nor think it right to be turned aside from the truth by any flattery, nor shun exile, knowing that the world is the fatherland of the wise man. She fears not want, for she knows that nothing is wanting to the wise man, since the whole world of riches is his. What is greater than the man that knows not how to be excited at the thought of money, and has a contempt for riches, and

Book Two

looks down as from some lofty vantage-ground on the desires of men? Men think that one who acts thus is more than man: Who is this, it says, and we will praise him. For wonderful things has he done in his life. (Sirach 31:9) Surely he ought to be admired who despises riches, seeing that most place them even before their own safety.

67. The rule of economy and the authority of self-restraint befits all, and most of all him who stands highest in honour; so that no love for his treasures may seize upon such a man, and that he who rules over free men may never become a slave to money. It is more seemly that in soul he should be superior to treasures, and in willing service be subject to his friends. For humility increases the regard in which one is held. It is praiseworthy and right for the chief of men to have no desire for filthy lucre in common with Syrian traders and Gilead merchants, nor to place all their hope of good in money, or to count up their daily gains and to calculate their savings like a hireling.

Chapter 15.

Of liberality. To whom it must chiefly be shown, and how men of slender means may show it by giving their service and counsel.

68. But if it is praiseworthy to have one's soul free from this failing, how much more glorious is it to gain the love of the people by liberality which is neither too freely shown to those who are unsuitable, nor too sparingly bestowed upon the needy.

69. There are many kinds of liberality. Not only can we distribute and give away food to those who need it from our own daily supply, so that they may sustain life; but we can also give advice and help to those who are ashamed to show their want openly, so long as the common supplies of the needy are not exhausted. I am now speaking of one set over some office. If he is a priest or almoner, let him inform the bishop of them, and not withhold the name of any he knows to be in any need, or to have lost their wealth and to be now reduced to want; especially if they have not fallen into this trouble owing to wastefulness in youth, but because of another's theft, or through loss of their inheritance from no fault of their own, so that they cannot now earn their daily bread.

70. The highest kind of liberality is, to redeem captives, to save them from the hands of their enemies, to snatch men from death, and, most of all, women from shame, to restore children to their parents, parents to their children, and, to give back a citizen to his country. This was recognized when Thrace and Illyria were so terribly devastated. How many captives were then for sale all over the world! Could one but call them together, their number would have surpassed that of a whole province. Yet there were some who would have sent back into slavery those whom the Church had redeemed. They themselves were harder than slavery itself to look askance at another's mercy. If they themselves (they said) had come to slavery, they would be slaves freely. If they had been sold, they would not refuse the service of slavery. They wished to undo the freedom of others, though they could not undo their own slavery, unless perchance it should please the buyer to receive his price again, whereby, however, slavery would not be simply undone but redeemed.

71. It is then a special quality of liberality to redeem captives, especially from barbarian enemies who are moved by no spark of human feeling to show mercy, except so far as avarice has preserved it with a view to redemption. It is also a great thing to take upon oneself another's debt, if the debtor cannot pay and is hard pressed to do so, and where the money is due by right and is only left unpaid through want. So, too, it is a sign of great liberality to bring up children, and to take care of orphans.

72. There are others who place in marriage maidens that have lost their parents, so as to preserve their chastity, and who help them not only with good wishes but also by a sum of money. There is also another kind of liberality which the Apostle teaches: If any that believes has widows let him relieve them, that the Church be not burdened by supplying them, that it may have enough for those that are widows indeed.
(1 Timothy 5:16)

73. Useful, then, is liberality of this sort; but it is not common to all. For there are many good men who have but slender means, and are content with little for their own use, and are not able to give help to lighten the poverty of others. However, another sort of kindness is ready to their hand, whereby they can help those poorer still. For there is a twofold liberality: one that gives actual assistance, that is, in

money; the other, which is busy in offering active help, is often much grander and nobler.

74. How much grander it was for Abraham to have recovered his captured son-in-law by his victorious arms, (Genesis 14:16) than if he had ransomed him! How much more usefully did holy Joseph help King Pharaoh by his counsel to provide for the future, than if he had offered him money! For money would not have bought back the fruitfulness of any one state; while he by his foresight kept the famine for five years (Genesis 41:53-57) from the whole of Egypt.

75. Money is easily spent; counsels can never be exhausted. They only grow the stronger by constant use. Money grows less and quickly comes to an end, and has failed even kindness itself; so that the more there are to whom one wants to give, the fewer one can help; and often one has not got what one thinks ought to be given to others. But as regards the offer of advice and active help, the more there are to spend it on, the more there seems to be, and the more it returns to its own source. The rich stream of prudence ever flows back upon itself, and the more it has reached out to, so much the more active becomes all that remains.

Chapter 16.

Due measure must be observed in liberality, that it may not be expended on worthless persons, when it is needed by worthier ones. However, alms are not to be given in too sparing and hesitating a way. One ought rather to follow the example of the blessed Joseph, whose prudence is commended at great length.

76. It is clear, then, that there ought to be due measure in our liberality, that our gifts may not become useless. Moderation must be observed, especially by priests, for fear that they should give away for the sake of ostentation, and not for justice' sake. Never was the greed of beggars greater than it is now. They come in full vigour, they come with no reason but that they are on the tramp. They want to empty the purses of the poor— to deprive them of their means of support. Not content with a little, they ask for more. In the clothes that cover them they seek a ground to urge their demands, and with lies about their lives they ask for further sums of money. If any one were to trust their tale too readily, he would quickly drain the fund which is meant to

serve for the sustenance of the poor. Let there be method in our giving, so that the poor may not go away empty nor the subsistence of the needy be done away and become the spoil of the dishonest. Let there be then such due measure that kindness may never be put aside, and true need never be left neglected.

77. Many pretend they have debts. Let the truth be looked into. They bemoan the fact that they have been stripped of everything by robbers. In such a case give credit only if the misfortune is apparent, or the person is well known; and then readily give help. To those rejected by the Church supplies must be granted if they are in want of food. He, then, that observes method in his giving is hard towards none, but is free towards all. We ought not only to lend our ears to hear the voices of those who plead, but also our eyes to look into their needs. Weakness calls more loudly to the good dispenser than the voice of the poor. It cannot always be that the cries of an importunate beggar will never extort more, but let us not always give way to impudence. He must be seen who does not see you. He must be sought for who is ashamed to be seen. He also that is in prison must come to your thoughts; another seized with sickness must present himself to your mind, as he cannot reach your ears.

78. The more people see your zeal in showing mercy, the more will they love you. I know many priests who had the more, the more they gave. For they who see a good dispenser give him something to distribute in his round of duty, sure that the act of mercy will reach the poor. If they see him giving away either in excess or too sparingly, they contemn either of these; in the one case because he wastes the fruits of another's labours by unnecessary payments, on the other hand because he hoards them in his money bags. As, then, method must be observed in liberality, so also at times it seems as though the spur must be applied. Method, then, so that the kindness one shows may be able to be shown day by day, and that we may not have to withdraw from a needful case what we have freely spent on waste. A spur, because money is better laid out in food for the poor than on a purse for the rich. We must take care lest in our money chests we shut up the welfare of the needy, and bury the life of the poor as it were in a sepulchre.

79. Joseph could have given away all the wealth of Egypt, and have spent the royal treasures; but he would not even seem to be wasteful of

Book Two

what was another's. He preferred to sell the grain rather than to give it to the hungry. For if he had given it to a few there would have been none for most. He gave good proof of that liberality whereby there was enough for all. He opened the storehouses that all might buy their grain supply, lest if they received it for nothing, they should give up cultivating the ground. For he who has the use of what is another's often neglects his own.

80. First of all, then, he gathered up their money, then their implements, last of all he acquired for the king all their rights to the ground. (Genesis 47:14-20) He did not wish to deprive all of them of their property, but to support them in it. He also imposed a general tax, that they might hold their own in safety. So pleasing was this to all from whom he had taken the land, that they looked on it, not as the selling of their rights, but as the recovery of their welfare. Thus they spoke: You have saved our lives, let us find grace in the sight of our Lord. (Genesis 47:25) For they had lost nothing of their own, but had received a new right. Nothing of what was useful to them had failed, for they had now gained it in perpetuity.

81. O noble man! who sought not for the fleeting glory of a needless bounty, but set up as his memorial the lasting benefits of his foresight. He acted so that the people should help themselves by their payments, and should not in their time of need seek help from others. For it was surely better to give up part of their crops than to lose the whole of their rights. He fixed the impost at a fifth of their whole produce, and thus showed himself clear-sighted in making provision for the future, and liberal in the tax he laid upon them. Never after did Egypt suffer from such a famine.

82. How splendidly he inferred the future. First, how acutely, when interpreting the royal dream, he stated the truth. This was the king's first dream. Seven heifers came up out of the river well-favoured and fat-fleshed, and they fed at the banks of the river. And other bullocks ill-favoured and lean-fleshed came up out of the river after the heifers, and fed near them on the very edge of the river. And these thin and wretched bullocks seemed to devour those others which were so fat and well-favoured. And this was the second dream. Seven fat ears full and good came up from the ground. And after them seven wretched ears, blasted with the wind and withered, endeavoured to take their

place. And it seemed that the barren and thin ears devoured the rich and fruitful ears.

83. This dream Joseph unfolded as follows: that the seven heifers were seven years, and the seven ears likewise were seven years—interpreting the times by the produce of cattle and crops. For both the calving of a heifer takes a year, and the produce of a crop fills out a whole year. And they came up out of the river just as days, years, and times pass by and flow along swiftly like the rivers. He therefore states that the seven earlier years of a rich land will be fertile and fruitful but the latter seven years will be barren and unfruitful, whose barrenness will eat up the richness of the former time. Wherefore he warns them to see that supplies of grain are got together in the fruitful years that they may help out the needs of the coming scarcity.

84. What shall we admire first? His powers of mind, with which he descended to the very resting-place of truth? Or his counsel, whereby he foresaw so great and lasting a need? Or his watchfulness or justice? By his watchfulness, when so high an office was given him, he gathered together such vast supplies; and through his justice he treated all alike. And what am I to say of his greatness of mind? For though sold by his brothers into slavery, (Genesis 37:28) he took no revenge for this wrong, but put an end to their want. What of his gentleness, whereby by a pious fraud he sought to gain the presence of his beloved brother whom, under pretence of a well-planned theft, he declared to have stolen his property, that he might hold him as a hostage of his love?

85. Whence it was deservedly said to him by his father: My son Joseph is enlarged, my son is enlarged, my younger son, my beloved. My God has helped you and blessed you with the blessing of heaven above and the blessing of the earth, the earth that has all things, on account of the blessings of your father and your mother. It has prevailed over the blessings of the everlasting hills and the desires of the eternal hills. And in Deuteronomy: You Who wast seen in the bush, that You may come upon the head of Joseph, upon his pate. Honoured among his brethren, his glory is as the firstling of his bullocks; his horns are like the horns of unicorns. With his horn he shall push the nations even to the ends of the earth. They are the ten thousands of Ephraim and the thousands of Manasseh. (Deuteronomy 33:16-17)

Book Two

Chapter 17.

What virtues ought to exist in him whom we consult. How Joseph and Paul were equipped with them.

86. Such, then, ought he to be who gives counsel to another, in order that he may offer himself as a pattern in all good works, in teaching, in trueness of character, in seriousness. Thus his words will be wholesome and irreproachable, his counsel useful, his life virtuous, and his opinions seemly.

87. Such was Paul, who gave counsel to virgins, (1 Corinthians 7:25) guidance to priests, so as to offer himself as a pattern for us to copy. Thus he knew how to be humble, as also Joseph did, who, though sprung from the noble family of the patriarchs, was not ashamed of his base slavery; rather he adorned it with his ready service, and made it glorious by his virtues. He knew how to be humble who had to go through the hands of both buyer and seller, and called them, Lord. Hear him as he humbles himself: My lord on my account knows not what is in his house, and he has committed all that he has to my hand, neither has he kept back anything from me but you, because you are his wife; how, then, can I do this great wickedness, and sin against God? (Genesis 39:8-9) Full of humility are his words, full, too, of chastity. Of humility, for he was obedient to his Lord; of an honourable spirit, for he was grateful; full, also, of chastity, for he thought it a terrible sin to be defiled by so great a crime.

88. Such, then, ought the man of counsel to be. He must have nothing dark, or deceptive, or false about him, to cast a shadow on his life and character, nothing wicked or evil to keep back those who want advice. For there are some things which one flies from, others which one despises. We fly from those things which can do harm, or can perfidiously and quietly grow to do us hurt, as when he whose advice we ask is of doubtful honour, or is desirous of money, so that a certain sum can make him change his mind. If a man acts unjustly, we fly from him and avoid him. A man that is a pleasure seeker and extravagant, although he does not act falsely, yet is avaricious and too fond of filthy lucre; such an one is despised. What proof of hard work, what fruits of labour, can he give who gives himself up to a sluggish and idle life, or what cares and anxieties ever enter his mind?

89. Therefore the man of good counsel says: I have learned in whatsoever state I am therewith to be content. (Philippians 4:11) For he knew that the root of all evils is the love of money, (1 Timothy 6:10) and therefore he was content with what he had, without seeking for what was another's. Sufficient for me, he says, is what I have; whether I have little or much, to me it is much. It seems as though he wanted to state it as clearly as possible. He makes use of these words: I am content, he says, with what I have. That means: I neither have want, nor have I too much. I have no want, for I seek nothing more. I have not too much, for I have it not for myself, but for the many. This is said with reference to money.

90. But he could have said these words about everything, for all that he had at the moment contented him; that is, he wanted no greater honour, he sought for no further services, he was not desirous of vainglory, nor did he look for gratitude where it was not due; but patient in labours, sure in his merits, he waited for the end of the struggle that he must needs endure. I know, he says, how to be abased. (Philippians 4:12) An untaught humility has no claim to praise, but only that which possesses modesty and a knowledge of self. For there is a humility that rests on fear, one, too, that rests on want of skill and ignorance. Therefore the Scripture says: He will save the humble in spirit. Gloriously, therefore, does he say: I know how to be abased; that is to say, where, in what moderation, to what end, in what duty, in which office. The Pharisee knew not how to be abased, therefore he was cast down. The publican knew, and therefore he was justified. (Luke 18:11)

91. Paul knew, too, how to abound, for he had a rich soul, though he possessed not the treasure of a rich man. He knew how to abound, for he sought no gift in money, but looked for fruit in grace. We can understand his words that he knew how to abound also in another way. For he could say again: O you Corinthians, our mouth is open unto you, our heart is enlarged. (2 Corinthians 6:14)

92. In all things he was accustomed both to be full and to be hungry. Blessed is he that knows how to be full in Christ. Not corporal, but spiritual, is that satiety which knowledge brings about. And rightly is there need of knowledge: For man lives not by bread alone, but by every word of God. (Deuteronomy 8:3) For he who knew how to be full also knew how to be hungry, so as to be always seeking something

new, hungering after God, thirsting for the Lord. He knew how to hunger, for he knew that the hungry shall eat. (Matthew 5:6) He knew, also, how to abound, and was able to abound, for he had nothing and yet possessed all things. (2 Corinthians 6:10)

Chapter 18.

We learn from the fact of the separation of the ten tribes from King Rehoboam what harm bad counsellors can do.

93. Justice, then, especially graces men that are set over any office; on the other hand, injustice fails them and fights against them. Scripture itself gives us an example, where it says, that when the people of Israel, after the death of Solomon, had asked his son Rehoboam to free their neck from their cruel yoke, and to lighten the harshness of his father's rule, he, despising the counsel of the old men, gave the following answer at the suggestion of the young men: He would add a burden to the yoke of his father, and change their lighter toils for harder.

94. Angered by this answer, the people said: We have no portion in David, nor inheritance in the son of Jesse. Return to your tents, O Israel. For we will not have this man for a prince or a leader over us. So, forsaken and deserted by the people, he could keep with him scarce two of the ten tribes for David's sake.

Chapter 19.

Many are won by justice and benevolence and courtesy, but all this must be sincere.

95. It is plain, then, that equity strengthens empires, and injustice destroys them. How could wickedness hold fast a kingdom when it cannot even rule over a single family? There is need, therefore, of the greatest kindness, so that we may preserve not only the government of affairs in general, but also the rights of individuals. Benevolence is of the greatest value; for it seeks to embrace all in its favours, to bind them to itself by fulfilling duties, and to pledge them to itself by its charm.

96. We have also said that courtesy of speech has great effect in winning favour. But we want it to be sincere and sensible, without flattery,

lest flattery should disgrace the simplicity and purity of our address. We ought to be a pattern to others not only in act but also in word, in purity, and in faith. What we wish to be thought, such let us be; and let us show openly such feelings as we have within us. Let us not say an unjust word in our heart that we think can be hid in silence, for He hears things said in secret Who made things secret, and knows the secrets of the heart, and has implanted feelings within. Therefore as though under the eyes of the Judge let us consider all we do as set forth in the light, that it may be manifest to all.

Chapter 20.

Familiarity with good men is very advantageous to all, especially to the young, as is shown by the example of Joshua and Moses and others. Further, those who are unlike in age are often alike in virtues, as Peter and John prove.

97. It is a very good thing to unite oneself to a good man. It is also very useful for the young to follow the guidance of great and wise men. For he who lives in company with wise men is wise himself; but he who clings to the foolish is looked on as a fool too. This friendship with the wise is a great help in teaching us, and also as giving a sure proof of our uprightness. Young men show very soon that they imitate those to whom they attach themselves. And this idea gains ground from the fact that in all their daily life they grow to be like those with whom they have enjoyed intercourse to the full.

98. Joshua the son of Nun became so great, because his union with Moses was the means not only of instructing him in a knowledge of the law, but also of sanctifying him to receive grace. When in His tabernacle the majesty of the Lord was seen to shine forth in its divine Presence, Joshua alone was in the tabernacle. When Moses spoke with God, Joshua too was covered by the sacred cloud. The priests and people stood below, and Joshua and Moses went up the mount to receive the law. All the people were within the camp; Joshua was without the camp in the tabernacle of witness. When the pillar of a cloud came down, and God spoke with Moses, he stood as a trusty servant beside him; and he, a young man, did not go out of the tabernacle, though the old men who stood afar off trembled at these divine wonders.

99. Everywhere, therefore, he alone kept close to holy Moses amid all these wondrous works and dread secrets. Wherefore it happens that he who had been his companion in this intercourse with God succeeded to his power. (Deuteronomy 34:9) Worthy surely was he to stand forth as a man who might stay the course of the river, and who might say: Sun, stand still, and delay the night and lengthen the day, as though to witness his victory. (Joshua 10:12-13) Why?— a blessing denied to Moses— he alone was chosen to lead the people into the promised land. A man he was, great in the wonders he wrought by faith, great in his triumphs. The works of Moses were of a higher type, his brought greater success. Either of these then aided by divine grace rose above all human standing. The one ruled the sea, the other heaven.

100. Beautiful, therefore, is the union between old and young. The one to give witness, the other to give comfort; the one to give guidance, the other to give pleasure. I pass by Lot, who when young clung to Abraham, as he was setting out. (Genesis 12:5) For some perhaps might say this arose rather owing to their relationship than from any voluntary action on his part. And what are we to say of Elijah and Elisha? Though Scripture has not in so many words stated that Elisha was a young man, yet we gather from it that he was the younger. In the Acts of the Apostles, Barnabas took Mark with him, and Paul took Silas (Acts 15:39-40) and Timothy (Acts 16:3) and Titus. (Titus 1:5)

101. We see also that duties were divided among them according to their superiority in anything. The elders took the lead in giving counsel, the younger in showing activity. Often, too, those who were alike in virtue but unlike in years were greatly rejoiced at their union, as Peter and John were. We read in the Gospel that John was a young man, even in his own words, though he was behind none of the elders in merits and wisdom. For in him there was a venerable ripeness of character and the prudence of the hoarhead. An unspotted life is the due of a good old age.

Chapter 21.

To defend the weak, or to help strangers, or to perform similar duties, greatly adds to one's worth, especially in the case of tried men. Whilst one gets great blame for love of money; wastefulness, also, in the case of priests is very much condemned.

102. The regard in which one is held is also very much enhanced when one rescues a poor man out of the hands of a powerful one, or saves a condemned criminal from death; so long as it can be done without disturbance, for fear that we might seem to be doing it rather for the sake of showing off than for pity's sake, and so might inflict severer wounds while desiring to heal slighter ones. But if one has freed a man who is crushed down by the resources and faction of a powerful person, rather than overwhelmed by the deserts of his own wickedness, then the witness of a great and high opinion grows strong.

103. Hospitality also serves to recommend many. For it is a kind of open display of kindly feelings: so that the stranger may not want hospitality, but be courteously received, and that the door may be open to him when he comes. It is most seemly in the eyes of the whole world that the stranger should be received with honour; that the charm of hospitality should not fail at our table; that we should meet a guest with ready and free service, and look out for his arrival.

104. This especially was Abraham's praise, for he watched at the door of his tent, that no stranger by any chance might pass by. He carefully kept a lookout, so as to meet the stranger, and anticipate him, and ask him not to pass by, saying: My lord, if I have found favour in your sight, pass not by your servant. (Genesis 18:3) Therefore as a reward for his hospitality, he received the gift of posterity.

105. Lot also, his nephew, (Genesis 19:20) who was near to him not only in relationship but also in virtue, on account of his readiness to show hospitality, turned aside the punishment of Sodom from himself and his family.

106. A man ought therefore to be hospitable, kind, upright, not desirous of what belongs to another, willing to give up some of his own rights if assailed, rather than to take away another's. He ought to avoid disputes, to hate quarrels. He ought to restore unity and the grace of

quietness. When a good man gives up any of his own rights, it is not only a sign of liberality, but is also accompanied by great advantages. To start with, it is no small gain to be free from the cost of a lawsuit. Then it also brings in good results, by an increase of friendship, from which many advantages rise. These become afterwards most useful to the man that can despise a little something at the time.

107. In all the duties of hospitality kindly feeling must be shown to all, but greater respect must be given to the upright. For Whosoever receives a righteous man, in the name of a righteous man, shall receive a righteous man's reward, (Matthew 10:41) as the Lord has said. Such is the favour in which hospitality stands with God, that not even the draught of cold water shall fail of getting a reward. (Matthew 10:42) You see that Abraham, in looking for guests, received God Himself to entertain. You see that Lot received the angels. (Genesis 19:3) And how do you know that when you receive men, thou dost not receive Christ? Christ may be in the stranger that comes, for Christ is there in the person of the poor, as He Himself says: I was in prison and you came to Me, I was naked and you clothed Me. (Matthew 25:36) .

108. It is sweet, then, to seek not for money but for grace. It is true that this evil has long ago entered into human hearts, so that money stands in the place of honour, and the minds of men are filled with admiration for wealth. Thus love of money sinks in and as it were dries up every kindly duty; so that men consider everything a loss which is spent beyond the usual amount. But even here the holy Scriptures have been on the watch against love of money, that it might prove no cause of hindrance, saying: Better is hospitality, even though it consists only of herbs. (Proverbs 15:17) And again: Better is bread in pleasantness with peace. (Proverbs 17:1) For the Scriptures teach us not to be wasteful, but liberal.

109. There are two kinds of free-giving, one arising from liberality, the other from wasteful extravagance. It is a mark of liberality to receive the stranger, to clothe the naked, to redeem the captives, to help the needy. It is wasteful to spend money on expensive banquets and much wine. Wherefore one reads: Wine is wasteful, drunkenness is abusive. (Proverbs 20:1) It is wasteful to spend one's own wealth merely for the sake of gaining the favour of the people. This they do who spend their inheritance on the games of the circus, or on theatrical pieces and gladiatorial shows, or even a combat of wild beasts, just to surpass the

fame of their forefathers for these things. All this that they do is but foolish, for it is not right to be extravagant in spending money even on good works.

110. It is a right kind of liberality to keep due measure towards the poor themselves, that one may have enough for more; and not to go beyond the right limit for the sake of winning favour. Whatever comes forth out of a pure sincere disposition, that is seemly. It is also seemly not to enter on unnecessary undertakings, nor to omit those that are needed.

111. But it befits the priest especially to adorn the temple of God with fitting splendour, so that the court of the Lord may be made glorious by his endeavours. He ought always to spend money as mercy demands. It behooves him to give to strangers what is right. This must not be too much, but enough; not more than, but as much as, kindly feeling demands, so that he may never seek another's favour at the expense of the poor, nor show himself as either too stingy or too free to the clergy. The one act is unkind, the other wasteful. It is unkind if money should be wanting for the necessities of those whom one ought to win back from their wretched employments. It is wasteful if there should be too much over for pleasure.

Chapter 22.
We must observe a right standard between too great mildness and excessive harshness. They who endeavour to creep into the hearts of others by a false show of mildness gain nothing substantial or lasting. This the example of Absalom plainly enough shows.

112. Moreover, due measure befits even our words and instructions, that it may not seem as though there was either too great mildness or too much harshness. Many prefer to be too mild, so as to appear to be good. But it is certain that nothing feigned or false can bear the form of true virtue; nay, it cannot even last. At first it flourishes, then, as time goes on, like a floweret it fades and passes away, but what is true and sincere has a deep root.

113. To prove by examples our assertion that what is feigned cannot last, but flourishing just for a time quickly fails, we will take one ex-

Book Two

ample of pretence and falsehood from that family, from which we have already drawn so many examples to show their growth in virtue.

114. Absalom was King David's son, known for his beauty, of splendid appearance and in the heyday of youth; so that no other such man as he was found in Israel. He was without a blemish from the sole of his foot to the crown of his head. He had for himself a chariot and horses and fifty men to run before him. He rose at early dawn and stood before the gate in the way, and whoever he knew to be seeking the judgment of the king, he called to himself, saying: From what city are you? And he answered: I your servant am of one of the tribes of Israel. And Absalom answered: Your words are good and right. Is there none given you by the king to hear you? Who will make me a judge? And whosoever will come unto me, that has need of judgment, I will give him justice. With such words he cajoled them. And when they came to make obeisance to him, stretching forth his hand he took hold of them and kissed them. So he turned the hearts of all to himself. For flattery of this sort quickly finds its way to touch the very depths of the heart.

115. Those spoilt and ambitious men chose what for a time seemed an honour to them, and was pleasing and enjoyable. But while that delay took place, which the prophet, being prudent above all, thought ought to intervene, they could no longer hold out or bear it. Then David having no doubt about the victory commended his son to those who went out to fight, so that they should spare him. He would not engage in the battle himself lest he should seem to be taking up arms against one who was still his son, though attempting to destroy his father.

116. It is clear, then, that those things are lasting and sound, which are true and grow out of a sincere and not a false heart. Those, however, which are brought about by pretence and adulation can never last for long.

Chapter 23.

The good faith of those who are easily bought over with money or flattery is a frail thing to trust to.

117. Who would suppose that those who are bought over to obedience by money, or those who are allured by adulation, would ever be faith-

ful to them? For the former are ever ready to sell themselves, while the latter cannot put up with a hard rule. They are easily won with a little adulation, but if one reproves them by a word, they murmur against it, they give one up, they go away with hostile feelings, they forsake one in anger. They prefer to rule rather than to obey. They think that those whom they ought to have placed over them ought to be subject to themselves, as though indebted to them by their kindness.

118. What man is there that thinks those will be faithful to himself, whom he believes he will have to bind to himself by money or flattery? For he who takes your money supposes that he is cheaply held, and looked down upon, unless the money is paid again and again. So he frequently expects his price; while the other, who is met with prayer and flattery, is always wanting to be asked.

Chapter 24.

We must strive for preferment only by right means. An office undertaken must be carried out wisely and with moderation. The inferior clergy should not detract from the bishop's reputation by feigned virtues; nor again, should the bishop be jealous of a cleric, but he should be just in all things and especially in giving judgment.

119. I think, then, that one should strive to win preferment, especially in the Church, only by good actions and with a right aim; so that there may be no proud conceit, no idle carelessness, no shameful disposition of mind, no unseemly ambition. A plain simplicity of mind is enough for everything, and commends itself quite sufficiently.

120. When in office, again, it is not right to be harsh and severe, nor may one be too easy; lest on the one hand we should seem to be exercising a despotic power, and on the other to be by no means filling the office we had taken up.

121. We must strive also to win many by kindnesses and duties that we can do, and to preserve the favour already shown us. For they will with good reason forget the benefits of former times if they are now vexed at some great wrong. For it often enough happens that those one has shown favour to and allowed to rise step by step, are driven away, if one decides in some unworthy way to put another before them. But it is seemly for a priest to show such favour in his kindnesses and his

decisions as to guard equity, and to show regard to the other clergy as to parents.

122. Those who once stood approved should not now become overbearing, but rather, as mindful of the grace they have received, stand firm in their humility. A priest ought not to be offended if either cleric or attendant or any ecclesiastic should win regard for himself, by showing mercy, or by fasting, or by uprightness of life, or by teaching and reading. For the grace of the Church is the praise of the teacher. It is a good thing that the work of another should be praised, if only it be done without any desire to boast. For each one should receive praise from the lips of his neighbour, and not from his own mouth, and each one should be commended by the work he has done, not merely by the wishes he had.

123. But if any one is disobedient to his bishop and wishes to exalt and upraise himself, and to overshadow his bishop's merits by a feigned appearance of learning or humility or mercy, he is wandering from the truth in his pride; for the rule of truth is, to do nothing to advance one's own cause whereby another loses ground, nor to use whatever good one has to the disgrace or blame of another.

124. Never protect a wicked man, nor allow the sacred things to be given over to an unworthy one; on the other hand, do not harass and press hard on a man whose fault is not clearly proved. Injustice quickly gives offense in every case, but especially in the Church, where equity ought to exist, where like treatment should be given to all, so that a powerful person may not claim the more, nor a rich man appropriate the more. For whether we be poor or rich, we are one in Christ. Let him that lives a holier life claim nothing more thereby for himself; for he ought rather to be the more humble for it.

125. In giving judgment let us have no respect of persons. Favour must be put out of sight, and the case be decided on its merits. Nothing is so great a strain on another's good opinion or confidence, as the fact of our giving away the cause of the weaker to the more powerful in any case that comes before us. The same happens if we are hard on the poor, while we make excuses for the rich man when guilty. Men are ready enough to flatter those in high positions, so as not to let them think themselves injured, or to feel vexed as though overthrown. But if you fear to give offense then do not undertake to give judgment. If you

are a priest or some cleric do not urge it. It is allowable for you to be silent in the matter, if it be a money affair, though it is always due to consistency to be on the side of equity. But in the cause of God, where there is danger to the whole Church, it is no small sin to act as though one saw nothing.

Chapter 25.

Benefits should be conferred on the poor rather than on the rich, for these latter either think a return is expected from them, or else they are angry at seeming to be indebted for such an action. But the poor man makes God the debtor in his place, and freely owns to the benefits he has received. To these remarks is added a warning to despise riches.

126. But what advantage is it to you to show favour to a rich man? Is it that he is more ready to repay one who loves him? For we generally show favour to those from whom we expect to receive a return of favour. But we ought to think far more of the weak and helpless, because we hope to receive, on behalf of him who has it not, a recompense from the Lord Jesus, Who in the likeness of a marriage feast (Luke 14:12-13) has given us a general representation of virtue. By this He bids us confer benefits rather on those who cannot give them to us in return, teaching us to bid to our feasts and meals, not those who are rich, but those that are poor. For the rich seem to be asked that they may prepare a banquet for us in return; the poor, as they have nothing wherewith to make return, when they receive anything, make the Lord to be our recompense Who has offered Himself as surety for the poor.

127. In the ordinary course of things, too, the conferring of a benefit on the poor is of more use than when it is conferred on the rich. The rich man scorns the benefit and is ashamed to feel indebted for a favour. Nay, moreover, whatever is offered to him he takes as due to his merits, as though only a just debt were paid him; or else he thinks it was but given because the giver expected a still greater return to be made him by the rich man. So, in accepting a kindness, the rich man, on that very ground, thinks that he has given more than he ever received. The poor man, however, though he has no money wherewith he can repay, at least shows his gratitude. And herein it is certain that he returns more than he received. For money is paid in coins, but gratitude never fails; money grows less by payment, but gratitude fails

when held back, and is preserved when given to others. Next— a thing the rich man avoids— the poor man owns that he feels bound by the debt. He really thinks help has been given him, not that it has been offered in return for his honour. He considers that his children have been again given him, that his life is restored and his family preserved. How much better, then, is it to confer benefits upon the good than on the ungrateful.

128. Wherefore the Lord said to His disciples: Take neither gold nor silver nor money. (Matthew 10:9) Whereby as with a sickle He cuts off the love of money that is ever growing up in human hearts. Peter also said to the lame man, who was always carried even from his mother's womb: Silver and gold have I none, but what I have give I you. In the Name of Jesus Christ of Nazareth, arise and walk. (Acts 3:6) So he gave not money, but he gave health. How much better it is to have health without money, than money without health! The lame man rose; he had not hoped for that: he received no money; though he had hoped for that. But riches are hardly to be found among the saints of the Lord, so as to become objects of contempt to them.

Chapter 26.

How long standing an evil love of money is, is plain from many examples in the Old Testament. And yet it is plain, too, how idle a thing the possession of money is.

129. But man's habits have so long applied themselves to this admiration of money, that no one is thought worthy of honour unless he is rich. This is no new habit. Nay, this vice (and that makes the matter worse) grew long years ago in the hearts of men. When the city of Jericho fell at the sound of the priests' trumpets, and Joshua the son of Nun gained the victory, he knew that the valour of the people was weakened through love of money and desire for gold. For when Achan had taken a garment of gold and two hundred shekels of silver and a golden ingot from the spoils of the ruined city, he was brought before the Lord, and could not deny the theft, but owned it. (Joshua 7:21)

130. Love of money, then, is an old, an ancient vice, which showed itself even at the declaration of the divine law; for a law was given to check it. (Exodus 20:17) On account of love of money Balak thought Balaam could be tempted by rewards to curse the people of our fathers.

(Numbers 22:17) Love of money would have won the day too, had not God bidden him hold back from cursing. Overcome by love of money Achan led to destruction all the people of the fathers. So Joshua the son of Nun, who could stay the sun from setting, could not stay the love of money in man from creeping on. At the sound of his voice the sun stood still, but love of money stayed not. When the sun stood still Joshua completed his triumph, but when love of money went on, he almost lost the victory.

131. Why? Did not the woman Delilah's love of money deceive Samson, the bravest man of all? (Judges 16:6) So he who had torn asunder the roaring lion with his hands; (Judges 14:6) who, when bound and handed over to his enemies, alone, without help, burst his bonds and slew a thousand of them; (Judges 15:14-15) who broke the cords interwoven with sinews as though they were but the slight threads of a net; he, I say, having laid his head on the woman's knee, was robbed of the decoration of his victory-bringing hair, that which gave him his might. Money flowed into the lap of the woman, and the favour of God forsook the man. (Judges 16:20)

132. Love of money, then, is deadly. Seductive is money, while it also defiles those who have it, and helps not those who have it not. Supposing that money sometimes is a help, yet it is only a help to a poor man who makes his want known. What good is it to him who does not long for it, nor seek it; who does not need its help and is not turned aside by pursuit of it? What good is it to others, if he who has it is alone the richer for it? Is he therefore more honourable because he has that whereby honour is often lost, because he has what he must guard rather than possess? We possess what we use, but what is beyond our use brings us no fruit of possession, but only the danger of watching.

Chapter 27.

In contempt of money there is the pattern of justice, which virtue bishops and clerics ought to aim at together with some others. A few words are added on the duty of not bringing an excommunication too quickly into force.

133. To come to an end; we know that contempt of riches is a form of justice, therefore we ought to avoid love of money, and strive with all

our powers never to do anything against justice, but to guard it in all our deeds and actions.

134. If we would please God, we must have love, we must be of one mind, we must follow humility, each one thinking the other higher than himself. This is true humility, when one never claims anything proudly for oneself, but thinks oneself to be the inferior. The bishop should treat the clerics and attendants, who are indeed his sons, as members of himself, and give to each one that duty for which he sees him to be fit.

135. Not without pain is a limb of the body cut off which has become corrupt. It is treated for a long time, to see if it can be cured with various remedies. If it cannot be cured, then it is cut off by a good physician. Thus it is a good bishop's desire to wish to heal the weak, to remove the spreading ulcers, to burn some parts and not to cut them off; and lastly, when they cannot be healed, to cut them off with pain to himself. Wherefore that beautiful rule of the Apostle stands forth brightly, that we should look each one, not on his own things, but on the things of others. (Philippians 2:4) In this way it will never come about that we shall in anger give way to our own feelings, or concede more than is right in favour to our own wishes.

Chapter 28.

Mercy must be freely shown even though it brings an odium of its own. With regard to this, reference is made to the well-known story about the sacred vessels which were broken up by Ambrose to pay for the redemption of captives; and very beautiful advice is given about the right use of the gold and silver which the Church possesses. Next, after showing from the action of holy Lawrence what are the true treasures of the Church, certain rules are laid down which ought to be observed in melting down and employing for such uses the consecrated vessels of the Church.

136. It is a very great incentive to mercy to share in others' misfortunes, to help the needs of others as far as our means allow, and sometimes even beyond them. For it is better for mercy's sake to take up a case, or to suffer odium rather than to show hard feeling. So I once brought odium on myself because I broke up the sacred vessels to redeem captives— a fact that could displease the Arians. Not that it

displeased them as an act, but as being a thing in which they could take hold of something for which to blame me. Who can be so hard, cruel, iron-hearted, as to be displeased because a man is redeemed from death, or a woman from barbarian impurities, things that are worse than death, or boys and girls and infants from the pollution of idols, whereby through fear of death they were defiled?

137. Although we did not act thus without good reason, yet we have followed it up among the people so as to confess and to add again and again that it was far better to preserve souls than gold for the Lord. For He Who sent the apostles without gold (Matthew 10:9) also brought together the churches without gold. The Church has gold, not to store up, but to lay out, and to spend on those who need. What necessity is there to guard what is of no good? Do we not know how much gold and silver the Assyrians took out of the temple of the Lord? Is it not much better that the priests should melt it down for the sustenance of the poor, if other supplies fail, than that a sacrilegious enemy should carry it off and defile it? Would not the Lord Himself say: Why did you suffer so many needy to die of hunger? Surely you had gold? Thou should have given them sustenance. Why are so many captives brought on the slave market, and why are so many unredeemed left to be slain by the enemy? It had been better to preserve living vessels than gold ones.

138. To this no answer could be given. For what would you say: I feared that the temple of God would need its ornaments? He would answer: The sacraments need not gold, nor are they proper to gold only— for they are not bought with gold. The glory of the sacraments is the redemption of captives. Truly they are precious vessels, for they redeem men from death. That, indeed, is the true treasure of the Lord which effects what His blood effected. Then, indeed, is the vessel of the Lord's blood recognized, when one sees in either redemption, so that the chalice redeems from the enemy those whom His blood redeemed from sin. How beautifully it is said, when long lines of captives are redeemed by the Church: These Christ has redeemed. Behold the gold that can be tried, behold the useful gold, behold the gold of Christ which frees from death, behold the gold whereby modesty is redeemed and chastity is preserved.

139. These, then, I preferred to hand over to you as free men, rather than to store up the gold. This crowd of captives, this company surely is more glorious than the sight of cups. The gold of the Redeemer

Book Two

ought to contribute to this work so as to redeem those in danger. I recognize the fact that the blood of Christ not only glows in cups of gold, but also by the office of redemption has impressed upon them the power of the divine operation.

140. Such gold the holy martyr Lawrence preserved for the Lord. For when the treasures of the Church were demanded from him, he promised that he would show them. On the following day he brought the poor together. When asked where the treasures were which he had promised, he pointed to the poor, saying: These are the treasures of the Church. And truly they were treasures, in whom Christ lives, in whom there is faith in Him. So, too, the Apostle says: We have this treasure in earthen vessels. (2 Corinthians 4:7) What greater treasures has Christ than those in whom He says He Himself lives? For thus it is written: I was hungry and you gave Me to eat, I was thirsty and you gave Me to drink, I was a stranger and you took Me in. (Matthew 25:35) And again: What you did to one of these, you did it unto Me. (Matthew 25:40) What better treasures has Jesus than those in which He loves to be seen?

141. These treasures Lawrence pointed out, and prevailed, for the persecutors could not take them away. Jehoiachim, who preserved his gold during the siege and spent it not in providing food, saw his gold carried off, and himself led into captivity. Lawrence, who preferred to spend the gold of the Church on the poor, rather than to keep it in hand for the persecutor, received the sacred crown of martyrdom for the unique and deep-sighted vigour of his meaning. Or was it perhaps said to holy Lawrence: Thou should not spend the treasures of the Church, or sell the sacred vessels?

142. It is necessary that every one should fill this office, with genuine good faith and clear-sighted forethought. If any one derives profit from it for himself it is a crime, but if he spends the treasures on the poor, or redeems captives, he shows mercy. For no one can say: Why does the poor man live? None can complain that captives are redeemed, none can find fault because a temple of the Lord is built, none can be angry because a plot of ground has been enlarged for the burial of the bodies of the faithful, none can be vexed because in the tombs of the Christians there is rest for the dead. In these three ways it is allowable to break up, melt down, or sell even the sacred vessels of the Church.

143. It is necessary to see that the mystic cup does not go out of the Church, lest the service of the sacred chalice should be turned over to base uses. Therefore vessels were first sought for in the Church which had not been consecrated to such holy uses. Then broken up and afterwards melted down, they were given to the poor in small payments, and were also used for the ransom of captives. But if new vessels fail, or those which never seem to have been used for such a holy purpose, then, as I have already said, I think that all might be put to this use without irreverence.

Chapter 29.

The property of widows or of all the faithful, that has been entrusted to the Church, ought to be defended though it brings danger to oneself. This is illustrated by the example of Onias the priest, and of Ambrose, bishop of Ticinum.

144. Great care must be taken that the property entrusted by widows remains inviolate. It should be guarded without causing complaint, not only if it belongs to widows, but to any one at all. For good faith must be shown to all, though the cause of the widow and orphans comes first.

145. So everything entrusted to the temple was preserved in the name of the widows alone, as we read in the book of the Maccabees. 2 Maccabbees iii For when information was given of the money, which Simon treacherously had told King Antiochus could be found in large quantities in the temple at Jerusalem, Heliodorus was sent to look into the matter. He came to the temple, and made known to the high priest his hateful information and the reason of his coming.

146. Then the priest said that only means for the maintenance of the widows and orphans was laid up there. And when Heliodorus would have gone to seize it, and to claim it on the king's behalf, the, priests cast themselves before the altar, after putting on their priestly robes, and with tears called on the living God Who had given them the law concerning trust-money to show Himself as guardian of His own commands. The changed look and colour of the high priest showed what grief of soul and anxiety and tension of mind were his. All wept, for the spot would fall into contempt, if not even in the temple of God safe and faithful guardianship could be preserved. Women with breasts

Book Two

girded, and virgins who usually were shut in, knocked at the doors. Some ran to the walls, others looked out of the windows, all raised their hands to heaven in prayer that God would stand by His laws.

147. But Heliodorus, undeterred by this, was eager to carry out his intention, and had already surrounded the treasury with his followers, when suddenly there appeared to him a dreadful horseman all glorious in golden armour, his horse also being adorned with costly ornaments. Two other youths also appeared in glorious might and wondrous beauty, in splendour and glory and beauteous array. They stood round him, and on either side beat the sacrilegious wretch, and gave him stroke after stroke without intermission. What more need I say? Shut in by darkness he fell to the ground, and lay there nearly dead with fear at this plain proof of divine power, nor had he any hope of safety left within him. Joy returned to those who were in fear, fear fell on those who were so proud before. And some of the friends of Heliodorus in their trouble besought Onias, asking life for him, since he was almost at his last breath.

148. When, therefore, the high priest asked for this, the same youths again appeared to Heliodorus, clad in the same garments, and said to him: Give thanks to Onias the high priest, for whose sake your life is granted you. But do thou, having experienced the scourge of God, go and tell your friends how much you have learned of the sanctity of the temple and the power of God. With these words they passed out of sight. Heliodorus then, his life having come back to him, offered a sacrifice to the Lord, gave thanks to the priest Onias, and returned with his army to the king, saying: If you have an enemy or one who is plotting against your power, send him there and you will receive him back well scourged.

149. Therefore, my sons, good faith must be preserved in the case of trust-money, and care, too, must be shown. Your service will glow the brighter if the oppression of a powerful man, which some widow or orphan cannot withstand, is checked by the assistance of the Church, and if you show that the command of the Lord has more weight with you than the favour of the rich.

150. You also remember how often we entered on a contest against the royal attacks, on behalf of the trust-money belonging to widows, yea, and to others as well. You and I shared this in common. I will also

mention the late case of the Church at Ticinum, which was in danger of losing the widow's trust-money that it had received. For when he who wanted to claim it on some imperial rescript demanded it, the clergy did not maintain their rights. For they themselves, having once been called to office and sent to intervene, now supposed that they could not oppose the emperor's orders. The plain words of the rescript were read, the orders of the chief officer of the court were there, he who was to act in the matter was at hand. What more was to be said? It was handed over.

151. However, after taking counsel with me, the holy bishop took possession of the rooms to which he knew that the widow's property had been carried. As it could not be carried away, it was all set down in writing. Later on it was again demanded on proof of the document. The emperor repeated the order, and would meet us himself in his own person. We refused. And when the force of the divine law, and a long list of passages and the danger of Heliodorus was explained, at length the emperor became reasonable. Afterwards, again, an attempt was made to seize it, but the good bishop anticipated the attempt and restored to the widow all he had received. So faith was preserved, but the oppression was no longer a cause for fear; for now it is the matter itself, not good faith, that is in danger.

Chapter 30.
The ending of the book brings an exhortation to avoid ill-will, and to seek prudence, faith, and the other virtues.

152. My sons, avoid wicked men, guard against the envious. There is this difference between a wicked and an envious man: the wicked man is delighted at his own good fortune, but the envious is tortured at the thought of another's. The former loves evil, the latter hates good. So he is almost more bearable who desires good for himself alone, than he who desires evil for all.

153. My sons, think before you act, and when you have thought long then do what you consider right. When the opportunity of a praiseworthy death is given let it be seized at once. Glory that is put off flies away and is not easily laid hold of again.

154. Love faith. For by his devotion and faith Josiah won great love for himself from his enemies. For he celebrated the Lord's passover when he was eighteen years old, as no one had done it before him. As then in zeal he was superior to those who went before him, so do ye, my sons, show zeal for God. Let zeal for God search you through, and devour you, so that each one of you may say: The zeal of your house has eaten me up. An apostle of Christ was called the zealot. (Luke 6:15) But why do I speak of an apostle? The Lord Himself said: The zeal of your house has eaten Me up. Let it then be real zeal for God, not mean earthy zeal, for that causes jealousy.

155. Let there be peace among you, which passes all understanding. Love one another. Nothing is sweeter than charity, nothing more blessed than peace. You yourselves know that I have ever loved you and do now love you above all others. As the children of one father you have become united under the bond of brotherly affection.

156. Whatsoever is good, that hold fast; and the God of peace and love be with you in the Lord Jesus, to Whom be honour and glory, dominion and might, together with the Holy Spirit, for ever and ever. Amen.

BOOK THREE

Chapter 1.

We are taught by David and Solomon how to take counsel with our own heart. Scipio is not to be accounted prime author of the saying which is ascribed to him. The writer proves what glorious things the holy prophets accomplished in their time of quiet, and shows, by examples of their and others' leisure moments, that a just man is never alone in trouble.

1. The prophet David taught us that we should go about in our heart as though in a large house; that we should hold converse with it as with some trusty companion. He spoke to himself, and conversed with himself, as these words show: I said, I will take heed to my ways. Solomon his son also said: Drink water out of your own vessels, and out of the springs of your wells; (Proverbs 5:15) that is: use your own counsel. For: Counsel in the heart of a man is as deep waters. (Proverbs 20:5) Let no stranger, it says, share it with you. Let the fountain of your water be your own, and rejoice with your wife who is yours from your youth. Let the loving hind and pleasant doe converse with you. (Proverbs 5:17-19)

2. Scipio, therefore, was not the first to know that he was not alone when he was alone, or that he was least at leisure when he was at leisure. For Moses knew it before him, who, when silent, was crying out; (Exodus 14:16) who, when he stood at ease, was fighting, nay, not merely fighting but triumphing over enemies whom he had not come near. So much was he at ease, that others held up his hands; yet he was no less active than others, for he with his hands at ease was overcoming the enemy, whom they that were in the battle could not conquer. (Exo-

dus 17:11) Thus Moses in his silence spoke, and in his ease laboured hard. And were his labours greater than his times of quiet, who, being in the mount for forty days, received the whole law? (Exodus 24:17) And in that solitude there was One not far away to speak with him. Whence also David says: I will hear what the Lord God will say within me. How much greater a thing is it for God to speak with any one, than for a man to speak with himself!

3. The apostles passed by and their shadows cured the sick. (Acts 5:15-16) Their garments were touched and health was granted.

4. Elijah spoke the word, and the rain ceased and fell not on the earth for three years and six months. Again he spoke, and the barrel of meal failed not, and the cruse of oil wasted not the whole time of that long famine.

5. But— as many delight in warfare— which is the most glorious, to bring a battle to an end by the strength of a great army, or, by merits before God alone? Elisha rested in one place while the king of Syria waged a great war against the people of our fathers, and was adding to its terrors by various treacherous plans, and was endeavouring to catch them in an ambush. But the prophet found out all their preparations, and being by the grace of God present everywhere in mental vigour, he told the thoughts of their enemies to his countrymen, and warned them of what places to beware. And when this was known to the king of Syria, he sent an army and shut in the prophet. Elisha prayed and caused all of them to be struck with blindness, and made those who had come to besiege him enter Samaria as captives.

6. Let us compare this leisure of his with that of others. Other men for the sake of rest are wont to withdraw their minds from business, and to retire from the company and companionship of men; to seek the retirement of the country or the solitude of the fields, or in the city to give their minds a rest and to enjoy peace and quietness. But Elisha was ever active. In solitude he divided Jordan on passing over it, so that the lower part flowed down, while the upper returned to its source. On Carmel he promises the woman, who so far had had no child, that a son now unhoped for should be born to her. He raises the dead to life, he corrects the bitterness of the food, and makes it to be sweet by mixing meal with it. Having distributed ten loaves to the people for food, he gathered up the fragments that were left after they had been filled.

He makes the iron head of the axe, which had fallen off and was sunk deep in the river Jordan, to swim by putting the wooden handle in the water. He changes leprosy for cleanness, drought for rain, famine for plenty.

7. When can the upright man be alone, since he is always with God? When is he left forsaken who is never separated from Christ? Who, it says, shall separate us from the love of Christ? I am confident that neither death nor life nor angel shall do so. (Romans 8:35), 38 And when can he be deprived of his labour who never can be deprived of his merits, wherein his labour receives its crown? By what places is he limited to whom the whole world of riches is a possession? By what judgment is he confined who is never blamed by any one? For he is as unknown yet well known, as dying and behold he lives, as sorrowful yet always rejoicing, as poor yet making many rich, as having nothing and yet possessing all things. For the upright man regards nothing but what is consistent and virtuous. And so although he seems poor to another, he is rich to himself, for his worth is taken not at the value of the things which are temporal, but of the things which are eternal.

Chapter 2.

The discussions among philosophers about the comparison between what is virtuous and what is useful have nothing to do with Christians. For with them nothing is useful which is not just. What are the duties of perfection, and what are ordinary duties? The same words often suit different things in different ways. Lastly, a just man never seeks his own advantage at the cost of another's disadvantage, but rather is always on the lookout for what is useful to others.

8. As we have already spoken about the two former subjects, wherein we discussed what is virtuous and what is useful, there follows now the question whether we ought to compare what is virtuous and useful together, and to ask which we must follow. For, as we have already discussed the matter as to whether a thing is virtuous or wicked, and in another place whether it is useful or useless, so here some think we ought to find out whether a thing is virtuous or useful.

9. I am induced to do this, lest I should seem to be allowing that these two are mutually opposed to one another, when I have already shown them to be one. For I said that nothing can be virtuous but what is use-

ful, and nothing can be useful but what is virtuous. For we do not follow the wisdom of the flesh, whereby the usefulness that consists in an abundance of money is held to be of most value, but we follow that wisdom which is of God, whereby those things which are greatly valued in this world are counted but as loss.

10. For this χατ⬚ρθωμα, which is duty carried out entirely and in perfection, starts from the true source of virtue. On this follows another, or ordinary duty. This shows by its name that no hard or extraordinary practice of virtue is involved, for it can be common to very many. The desire to save money is the usual practice with many. To enjoy a well-prepared banquet and a pleasant meal is a general habit; but to fast or to use self-restraint is the practice of but few, and not to be desirous of another's goods is a virtue rarely found. On the other hand, to wish to deprive another of his property— and not to be content with one's due— here one will find many to keep company with one. Those (the philosopher would say) are primary duties— these ordinary. The primary are found but with few, the ordinary with the many.

11. Again, the same words often have a different meaning. For instance, we call God good and a man good; but it bears in each case quite a different meaning. We call God just in one sense, man in another. So, too, there is a difference in meaning when we call God wise and a man wise. This we are taught in the Gospel: Be perfect even as your Father Who is in heaven is perfect. (Matthew 5:48) I read again that Paul was perfect and yet not perfect. For when he said: Not as though I had already attained, either were already perfect; but I follow after, if that I may apprehend it. (Philippians 3:12) Immediately he added: We, then, that are perfect. (Philippians 3:15) There is a twofold form of perfection, the one having but ordinary, the other the highest worth. The one availing here, the other hereafter. The one in accordance with human powers, the other with the perfection of the world to come. But God is just through all, wise above all, perfect in all.

12. There is also diversity even among men themselves. Daniel, of whom it was said: Who is wiser than Daniel? (Ezekiel 28:3) was wise in a different sense to what others are. The same may be said of Solomon, who was filled with wisdom, above all the wisdom of the ancients, and more than all the wise men of Egypt. To be wise as men are in general is quite a different thing to being really wise. He who is ordinarily wise is wise for temporal matters, is wise for himself, so as to deprive

another of something and get it for himself. He who is really wise does not know how to regard his own advantage, but looks with all his desire to that which is eternal, and to that which is seemly and virtuous, seeking not what is useful for himself, but for all.

13. Let this, then, be our rule, so that we may never go wrong between two things, one virtuous, the other useful. The upright man must never think of depriving another of anything, nor must he ever wish to increase his own advantage to the disadvantage of another. This rule the Apostle gives you, saying: All things are lawful, but all things are not expedient; all things are lawful, but all things edify not. Let no man seek his own, but each one another's. (1 Corinthians 10:23-24) That is: Let no man seek his own advantage, but another's; let no man seek his own honour, but another's. Wherefore he says in another place: Let each esteem other better than themselves, looking not each one to his own things, but to the things of others. (Philippians 2:3-4)

14. And let no one seek his own favour or his own praise, but another's. This we can plainly see declared in the book of Proverbs, where the Holy Spirit says through Solomon: My son, if you be wise, be wise for yourself and your neighbours; but if you turn out evil, thou alone shall bear it. (Proverbs 9:12) The wise man gives counsel to others, as the upright man does, and shares with him in wearing the form of either virtue.

Chapter 3.

The rule given about not seeking one's own gain is established, first by the examples of Christ, next by the meaning of the word, and lastly by the very form and uses of our limbs. Wherefore the writer shows what a crime it is to deprive another of what is useful, since the law of nature as well as the divine law is broken by such wickedness. Further, by its means we also lose that gift which makes us superior to other living creatures; and lastly, through it civil laws are abused and treated with the greatest contempt.

15. If, then, any one wishes to please all, he must strive in everything to do, not what is useful for himself, but what is useful for many, as also Paul strove to do. For this is to be conformed to the image of Christ, (Romans 8:29) namely, when one does not strive for what is another's, and does not deprive another of something so as to gain it for

oneself. For Christ our Lord, (Philippians 2:6-7) though He was in the form of God, emptied Himself so as to take on Himself the form of man, which He wished to enrich with the virtue of His works. Will you, then, spoil him whom Christ has put on? Will you strip him whom Christ has clothed? For this is what you are doing when thou dost attempt to increase your own advantage at another's loss.

16. Think, O man, from whence you have received your name— even from the earth, which takes nothing from any one, but gives freely to all, and supplies varied produce for the use of all living things. Hence humanity is called a particular and innate virtue in man, for it assists its partner.

17. The very form of your body and the uses of your limbs teach you this. Can one limb claim the duties of another? Can the eye claim for itself the duties of the ear; or the mouth the duties of the eye; or the hand the service of the feet; or the feet that of the hands? Nay, the hands themselves, both left and right, have different duties to do, so that if one were to change the use of either, one would act contrary to nature. We should have to lay aside the whole man before we could change the service of the various members: as if, for instance, we were to try to take food with the left hand, or to perform the duties of the left hand with the right, so as to remove the remains of food— unless, of course, need demanded it.

18. Imagine for a moment, and give to the eye the power to withdraw the understanding from the head, the sense of hearing from the ears, the power of thought from the mind, the sense of smell from the nose, the sense of taste from the mouth, and then to assume them itself, would it not at once destroy the whole order of nature? Wherefore the Apostle says well: If the whole body were an eye, where were the hearing? If the whole were hearing, where were the smelling? (1 Corinthians 12:17) So, then, we are all one body, though with many members, all necessary to the body. For no one member can say of another: I have no need of you. For those members which seem to be more feeble are much more necessary and require greater care and attention. And if one member suffers, all the members suffer with it. (1 Corinthians 12:26)

19. So we see how grave a matter it is to deprive another, with whom we ought rather to suffer, of anything, or to act unfairly or injuriously

towards one to whom we ought to give a share in our services. This is a true law of nature, which binds us to show all kindly feeling, so that we should all of us in turn help one another, as parts of one body, and should never think of depriving another of anything, seeing it is against the law of nature even to abstain from giving help. We are born in such a way that limb combines with limb, and one works with another, and all assist each other in mutual service. But if one fails in its duty, the rest are hindered. If, for instance, the hand tears out the eye, has it not hindered the use of its work? If it were to wound the foot, how many actions would it not prevent? But how much worse is it for the whole man to be drawn aside from his duty than for one of the members only! If the whole body is injured in one member, so also is the whole community of the human race disturbed in one man. The nature of mankind is injured, as also is the society of the holy Church, which rises into one united body, bound together in oneness of faith and love. Christ the Lord, also, Who died for all, will grieve that the price of His blood was paid in vain.

20. Why, the very law of the Lord teaches us that this rule must be observed, so that we may never deprive another of anything for the sake of our own advantage. For it says: Remove not the bounds which your fathers have set. (Proverbs 22:28) It bids a neighbour's ox to be brought back if found wandering. (Exodus 23:4) It orders a thief to be put to death. (Exodus 22:2) It forbids the labourer to be deprived of his hire, (Leviticus 19:13) and orders money to be returned without usury. (Deuteronomy 23:19) It is a mark of kindly feeling to help him who has nothing, but it is a sign of a hard nature to extort more than one has given. If a man has need of your assistance because he has not enough of his own wherewith to repay a debt, is it not a wicked thing to demand under the guise of kindly feeling a larger sum from him who has not the means to pay off a less amount? Thou dost but free him from debt to another, to bring him under your own hand; and you call that human kindliness which is but a further wickedness.

21. It is in this very matter that we stand before all other living creatures, for they do not understand how to do good. Wild beasts snatch away, men share with others. Wherefore the Psalmist says: The righteous shows mercy and gives. There are some, however, to whom the wild beasts do good. They feed their young with what they get, and the birds satisfy their brood with food; but to men alone has it been given to feed all as though they were their own. That is so in accordance

with the claims of nature. And if it is not lawful to refuse to give, how is it lawful to deprive another? And do not our very laws teach us the same? They order those things which have been taken from others with injury to their persons or property to be restored with additional recompense; so as to check the thief from stealing by the penalty, and by the fine to recall him from his ways.

22. Suppose, however, that some one did not fear the penalty, or laughed at the fine, would that make it a worthy thing to deprive another of his own? That would be a mean vice and suited only to the lowest of the low. So contrary to nature is it, that while want might seem to drive one to it, yet nature could never urge it. And yet we find secret theft among slaves, open robbery among the rich.

23. But what so contrary to nature as to injure another for our own benefit? The natural feelings of our own hearts urge us to keep on the watch for all, to undergo trouble, to do work for all. It is considered also a glorious thing for each one at risk to himself to seek the quiet of all, and to think it far more thankworthy to have saved his country from destruction than to have kept danger from himself. We must think it a far more noble thing to labour for our country than to pass a quiet life at ease in the full enjoyment of leisure.

Chapter 4.

As it has been shown that he who injures another for the sake of his own advantage will undergo terrible punishment at the hand of his own conscience, it is referred that nothing is useful to one which is not in the same way useful to all. Thus there is no place among Christians for the question propounded by the philosophers about two shipwrecked persons, for they must show love and humility to all.

24. Hence we infer that a man who guides himself according to the ruling of nature, so as to be obedient to her, can never injure another. If he injures another, he violates nature, nor will he think that what he has gained is so much an advantage as a disadvantage. And what punishment is worse than the wounds of the conscience within? What judgment harder than that of our hearts, whereby each one stands convicted and accuses himself of the injury that he has wrongfully done against his brother? This the Scriptures speak of very plainly, saying: Out of the mouth of fools there is a rod for wrong-doing. (Proverbs 14:3)

On the Duties of the Clergy

Folly, then, is condemned because it causes wrong-doing. Ought we not rather to avoid this, than death, or loss, or want, or exile, or sickness? Who would not think some blemish of body or loss of inheritance far less than some blemish of soul or loss of reputation?

25. It is clear, then, that all must consider and hold that the advantage of the individual is the same as that of all, and that nothing must be considered advantageous except what is for the general good. For how can one be benefited alone? That which is useless to all is harmful. I certainly cannot think that he who is useless to all can be of use to himself. For if there is one law of nature for all, there is also one state of usefulness for all. And we are bound by the law of nature to act for the good of all. It is not, therefore, right for him who wishes the interests of another to be considered according to nature, to injure him against the law of nature.

26. For if those who run in a race are, as one hears, instructed and warned each one to win the race by swiftness of foot and not by any foul play, and to hasten on to victory by running as hard as they can, but not to dare to trip up another or push him aside with their hand, how much more in the course of this life ought the victory to be won by us, without falseness to another and cheating?

27. Some ask whether a wise man ought in case of a shipwreck to take away a plank from an ignorant sailor? Although it seems better for the common good that a wise man rather than a fool should escape from shipwreck, yet I do not think that a Christian, a just and a wise man, ought to save his own life by the death of another; just as when he meets with an armed robber he cannot return his blows, lest in defending his life he should stain his love toward his neighbour. The verdict on this is plain and clear in the books of the Gospel. Put up your sword, for every one that takes the sword shall perish with the sword. (Matthew 26:52) What robber is more hateful than the persecutor who came to kill Christ? But Christ would not be defended from the wounds of the persecutor, for He willed to heal all by His wounds.

28. Why do you consider yourself greater than another, when a Christian man ought to put others before himself, to claim nothing for himself, usurp no honours, claim no reward for his merits? Why, next, are you not wont to bear your own troubles rather than to destroy another's advantage? For what is so contrary to nature as not to be

content with what one has or to seek what is another's, and to try to get it in shameful ways. For if a virtuous life is in accordance with nature— for God made all things very good— then shameful living must be opposed to it. A virtuous and a shameful life cannot go together, since they are absolutely severed by the law of nature.

Chapter 5.

The upright does nothing that is contrary to duty, even though there is a hope of keeping it secret. To point this out the tale about the ring of Gyges was invented by the philosophers. Exposing this, he brings forward known and true examples from the life of David and John the Baptist.

29. To lay down here already the result of our discussion, as though we had already ended it, we declare it a fixed rule, that we must never aim at anything but what is virtuous. The wise man does nothing but what can be done openly and without falseness, nor does he do anything whereby he may involve himself in any wrong-doing, even where he may escape notice. For he is guilty in his own eyes, before being so in the eyes of others; and the publicity of his crime does not bring him more shame than his own consciousness of it. This we can show, not by the made-up stories which philosophers use, but from the true examples of good men.

30. I need not, therefore, imagine a great chasm in the earth, which had been loosened by heavy rains, and had afterwards burst asunder, as Plato does. For he makes Gyges descend into that chasm, and to meet there that iron horse of the fable that had doors in its sides. When these doors were opened, he found a gold ring on the finger of a dead man, whose corpse lay there lifeless. He desiring the gold took away the ring. But when he returned to the king's shepherds, to whose number he belonged, by chance having turned the stone inwards towards the palms of his hands, he saw all, yet was seen by none. Then when he turned the ring to its proper position, he was again seen by all. On becoming conscious of this strange power, by the use of the ring he committed adultery with the queen, killed the king, and took possession of the kingdom after slaying all the rest, who he thought should be put to death, so that they might be no hindrance to him.

31. Give, says Plato, this ring to a wise man, that when he commits a fault he may by its help remain unnoticed; yet he will be none the more free from the stain of sin than if he could not be hid. The hiding-place of the wise lies not in the hope of impunity but in his own innocency. Lastly, the law is not laid down for the just but for the unjust. (1 Timothy 1:9) For the just has within himself the law of his mind, and a rule of equity and justice. Thus he is not recalled from sin by fear of punishment, but by the rule of a virtuous life.

32. Therefore, to return to our subject, I will now bring forward, not false examples for true, but true examples in place of false. For why need I imagine a chasm in the earth, and an iron horse and a gold ring found on the fingers of a dead man; and say that such was the power of this ring, that he who wore it could appear at his own will, but if he did not wish to be seen, he could remove himself out of the sight of those who stood by, so as to seem to be away. This story, of course, is meant to answer the question whether a wise man, on getting the opportunity of using that ring so as to be able to hide his crimes, and to obtain a kingdom,— whether, I say, a wise man would be unwilling to sin and would consider the stain of sin far worse than the pains of punishment, or whether he would use it for doing wickedness in the hope of not being found out? Why, I say, should I need the pretence of a ring, when I can show from what has been done that a wise man, on seeing he would not only be undetected in his sin, but would also gain a kingdom if he gave way to it, and who, on the other hand, noted danger to his own safety if he did not commit the crime, yet chose to risk his own safety so as to be free from crime, rather than to commit the crime and so gain the kingdom.

33. When David fled from the face of King Saul, because the king was seeking him in the desert with three thousand chosen men to put him to death, he entered the king's camp and found him sleeping. There he not only did him no injury, but actually guarded him from being slain by any who had entered with him. For when Abishai said to him: The Lord has delivered your enemy into your hand this day, now therefore I will slay him, he answered: Destroy him not, for who can stretch forth his hand against the Lord's anointed, and be guiltless? And he added: As the Lord lives, unless the Lord shall smite him, or his day shall come to die, or he shall die in battle, and it be laid to me, the Lord forbid that I should stretch out my hand against the Lord's anointed.

34. Therefore he did not suffer him to be slain, but removed only his spear, which stood by his head, and his cruse of water. Then, while all were sleeping, he left the camp and went across to the top of the hill, and began to reproach the royal attendants, and especially their general Abner, for not keeping faithful watch over their lord and king. Next, he showed them where the king's spear and cruse were which had stood at his head. And when the king called to him, he restored the spear, and said: The Lord render to every man his righteousness and faithfulness, for the Lord delivered you into my hand, but I would not avenge myself on the Lord's anointed. Even while he said this, he feared his plots and fled, changing his place in exile. However, he never put safety before innocency, seeing that when a second opportunity was given him of killing the king, he would not use the chance that came to him, and which put in his reach certain safety instead of fear, and a kingdom instead of exile.

35. Where was the use of the ring in John's case, (Matthew 14:3) who would not have been put to death by Herod if he had kept silence? He could have kept silence before him so as to be both seen and yet not killed. But because he not only could not endure to sin himself to protect his own safety, but could not bear and endure even another's sin, he brought about the cause of his own death. Certainly none can deny that he might have kept silence, who in the case of Gyges deny that he could have remained invisible by the help of the ring.

36. But although that fable has not the force of truth, yet it has this much to go upon, that if an upright man could hide himself, yet he would avoid sin just as though he could not conceal himself; and that he would not hide his person by putting on a ring, but his life by putting on Christ. As the Apostle says: Our life is hid with Christ in God. (Colossians 3:3) Let, then, no one here strive to shine, let none show pride, let none boast. Christ willed not to be known here, He would not that His Name should be preached in the Gospel while He lived on earth. He came to lie hidden from this world. Let us therefore likewise hide our life after the example of Christ, let us shun boastfulness, let us not desire to be made known. It is better to live here in humility, and there in glory. When Christ, it says, shall appear, then shall we also appear with Him in glory. (Colossians 3:4)

Chapter 6.

We ought not to allow the idea of profit to get hold of us. What excuses they make who get their gains by selling grain, and what answer ought to be made to them. In connection with this certain parables from the Gospels and some of the sayings of Solomon are set before our eyes.

37. Let not, therefore, expediency get the better of virtue, but virtue of expediency. By expediency here I mean what is accounted so by people generally. Let love of money be destroyed, let lust die. The holy man says that he has never been engaged in business. For to get an increase in price is a sign not of simplicity but of cunning. Elsewhere it says: He that seeks a high price for his grain is cursed among the people. (Proverbs 11:26)

38. Plain and definite is the statement, leaving no room for debate, such as a disputatious kind of speaking is wont to give, when one maintains that agriculture is considered praiseworthy by all; that the fruits of the earth are easily grown; that the more a man has sown, the greater will be his meed of praise; further, that the richer returns of his active labours are not gained by fraud, and that carelessness and disregard for an uncultivated soil are wont to be blamed.

39. I have ploughed, he says, carefully. I have sown freely. I have tilled actively. I have gathered good increase. I have stored it anxiously, saved it faithfully, and guarded it with care. Now in a time of famine I sell it, and come to the help of the hungry. I sell my own grain, not another's. And for no more than others, nay, even at a less price. What fraud is there here, when many would come to great danger if they had nothing to buy? Is industry to be made a crime? Or diligence to be blamed? Or foresight to be abused? Perhaps he may even say: Joseph collected grain in a time of abundance, and sold it when it was dear. Is any one forced to buy it at too dear a price? Is force employed against the buyer? The opportunity to buy is afforded to all, injury is inflicted on none.

40. When this has been said, and one man's ideas have carried him so far, another rises and says: Agriculture is good indeed, for it supplies fruits for all, and by simple industry adds to the richness of the earth without any cheating or fraud. If there is any error, the loss is the greater, for the better a man sows, the better he will reap. If he has

Book Three

sown the pure grain of wheat, he gathers a purer and cleaner harvest. The fruitful earth returns what she has received in manifold measure. A good field returns its produce with interest.

41. You must expect payment for your labour from the crops of the fruitful land, and must hope for a just return from the fruitfulness of the rich earth. Why do you use the industry of nature and make a cheat of it? Why do you grudge for the use of men what is grown for all? Why lessen the abundance for the people? Why make want your aim? Why make the poor long for a barren season? For when they do not feel the benefits of a fruitful season, because you are putting up the price, and art storing up the grain, they would far rather that nothing should be produced, than that you should do business at the expense of other people's hunger. You make much of the lack of grain, the small supply of food. You groan over the rich crops of the soil; you mourn the general plenty, and bewailest the garners full of grain; you are on the lookout to see when the crop is poor and the harvest fails. You rejoice that a curse has smiled upon your wishes, so that none should have their produce. Then you rejoice that your harvest has come. Then you collect wealth from the misery of all, and callest this industry and diligence, when it is but cunning shrewdness and an adroit trick of the trade. You call it a remedy, when it is but a wicked contrivance. Shall I call this robbery or only gain? These opportunities are seized as though seasons for plunder, wherein, like some cruel waylayer, you may fall upon the stomachs of men. The price rises higher as though by the mere addition of interest, but the danger to life is increased too. For then the interest of the stored-up crops grows higher. As a usurer you hide up your grain, as a seller you put it up for auction. Why do you wish evil to all, because the famine will grow worse, as though no grain should be left, as though a more unfruitful year should follow? Your gain is the public loss.

42. Holy Joseph opened the garners to all; he did not shut them up. He did not try to get the full price of the year's produce, but assigned it for a yearly payment. He took nothing for himself, but, so far as famine could be checked for the future, he made his arrangements with careful foresight.

43. You have read how the Lord Jesus in the Gospel speaks of that grain-dealer who was looking out for a high price, whose possessions brought him in rich fruits, but who, as though still in need, said: What

shall I do? I have no room where to bestow my goods. I will pull down my barns and build greater, (Luke 12:17) though he could not know whether in the following night his soul would not be demanded of him. He knew not what to do, he seemed to be in doubt, just as though he were in want of food. His barns could not take in the year's supply, and yet he thought he was in need.

44. Rightly, therefore, Solomon says: He that withholds grain shall leave it for the nations, not for his heirs, for the gains of avarice have nothing to do with the rights of succession. That which is not rightfully got together is scattered as though by a wind by outsiders that seize it. And he added: He who grasps at the year's produce is cursed among the people, but blessing shall be his that imparts it. You see, then, what is said of him who distributes the grain, but not of him that seeks for a high price. True expediency does not therefore exist where virtue loses more than expediency gains.

Chapter 7.

Strangers must never be expelled the city in a time of famine. In this matter the noble advice of a Christian sage is adduced, in contrast to which the shameful deed committed at Rome is given. By comparing the two it is shown that the former is combined with what is virtuous and useful, but the latter with neither.

45. But they, too, who would forbid the city to strangers cannot have our approval. They would expel them at the very time when they ought to help, and separate them from the trade of their common parent. They would refuse them a share in the produce meant for all, and avert the intercourse that has already begun; and they are unwilling, in a time of necessity, to give those with whom they have enjoyed their rights in common, a share in what they themselves have. Beasts do not drive out beasts, yet man shuts out man. Wild beasts and animals consider food which the earth supplies to be common to all. They all give assistance to those like themselves; and man, who ought to think nothing human foreign to himself, fights against his own.

46. How much better did he act who, having already reached an advanced age, when the city was suffering from famine, and, as is common in such cases, the people demanded that strangers should be forbidden the city, having the office of the prefectship of the city,

which is higher than the rest, called together the officials and richer men, and demanded that they should take counsel for the public welfare. He said that it was as cruel a thing for the strangers to be expelled as for one man to be cast off by another, and to be refused food when dying. We do not allow our dogs to come to our table and leave them unfed, yet we shut out a man. How unprofitable, again, it is for the world that so many people perish, whom some deadly plague carries off. How unprofitable for their city that so large a number should perish, who were wont to be helpful either in paying contributions or in carrying on business. Another's hunger is profitable to no man, nor to put off the day of help as long as possible and to do nothing to check the want. Nay more, when so many of the cultivators of the soil are gone, when so many labourers are dying, the grain supplies will fail for the future. Shall we then expel those who are wont to supply us with food, are we unwilling to feed in a time of need those who have fed us all along? How great is the assistance which they supply even at this time. Not by bread alone does man live. (Deuteronomy 8:3) They are even our own family; many of them even are our own kindred. Let us make some return for what we have received.

47. But perhaps we fear that want may increase. First of all, I answer, mercy never fails, but always finds means of help. Next, let us make up for the grain supplies which are to be granted to them, by a subscription. Let us put that right with our gold. And, again, must we not buy other cultivators of the soil if we lose these? How much cheaper is it to feed than to buy a working-man. Where, too, can one obtain, where find a man to take the place of the former? And suppose one finds him, do not forget that, with an ignorant man used to different ways, one may fill up the place in point of numbers, but not as regards the work to be done.

48. Why need I say more? When the money was supplied grain was brought in. So the city's abundance was not diminished, and yet assistance was given to the strangers. What praise this act won that holy man from God! What glory among men! He, indeed, had won an honoured name, who, pointing to the people of a whole province, could truly say to the emperor: All these I have preserved for you; these live owing to the kindness of the senate; these your council has snatched from death!

49. How much more expedient was this than that which was done lately at Rome. There from that widely extended city were those expelled who had already passed most of their life in it. In tears they went forth with their children, for whom as being citizens they bewailed the exile, which, as they said, ought to be averted; no less did they grieve over the broken bonds of union, the severed ties of relationship. And yet a fruitful year had smiled upon us. The city alone needed grain to be brought into it. It could have got help, if it had sought grain from the Italians whose children they were driving out. Nothing is more shameful than to expel a man as a foreigner, and yet to claim his services as though he belonged to us. How can you expel a man who lives on his own produce? How can you expel him who supplies you with food? You retain your servant, and thrust out your kindred! You take the grain, but show no good feeling! You take food by force, but do not show gratitude!

50. How wretched this is, how useless! For how can that be expedient which is not seemly. Of what great supplies from her corporations has Rome at times been deprived, yet she could not dismiss them and yet escape a famine, while waiting for a favourable breeze, and the provisions in the hoped-for ships.

51. How far more virtuous and expedient was that first-mentioned management! For what is so seemly or virtuous as when the needy are assisted by the gifts of the rich, when food is supplied to the hungry, when daily bread fails none? What so advantageous as when the cultivators are kept for the land, and the country people do not perish?

52. What is virtuous, then, is also expedient, and what is expedient is virtuous. On the other hand, what is not expedient is unseemly, and what is unseemly is also not expedient.

Chapter 8.

That those who put what is virtuous before what is useful are acceptable to God is shown by the example of Joshua, Caleb, and the other spies.

53. When could our fathers ever have thrown off their servitude, unless they had believed that it was not only shameful but even useless to serve the king of Egypt?

54. Joshua, also, and Caleb, when sent to spy out the land, brought back the news that the land was indeed rich, but that it was inhabited by very fierce nations. (Numbers 13:27-28) The people, terrified at the thought of war, refused to take possession of their land. Joshua and Caleb, who had been sent as spies, tried to persuade them that the land was fruitful. They thought it unseemly to give way before the heathen; they chose rather to be stoned, which is what the people threatened, than to recede from their virtuous standpoint. The others kept dissuading, the people exclaimed against it, saying they would have to fight against cruel and terrible nations; that they would fall in battle, and their wives and children would be left for a prey. (Numbers 14:3)

55. The anger of the Lord burst forth, so that He would kill all, but at the prayer of Moses He softened His judgment and put off His vengeance, knowing that He had already sufficiently punished those who were faithless, even if He spared them meanwhile and did not slay the unbelievers. However, He said (Numbers 14:29) they should not come to that land which they had refused, as a penalty for their unbelief; but their children and wives, who had not murmured, and who, owing to their sex and age, were guiltless, should receive the promised inheritance of that land. So the bodies of those of twenty years old and upwards fell in the desert. The punishment of the rest was put aside. But they who had gone up with Joshua, and had thought fit to dissuade the people, died immediately of a great plague. (Numbers 14:37) Joshua and Caleb (Joshua 14:6) entered the land of promise together with those who were innocent by reason of age or sex.

56. The better part, therefore, preferred glory to safety; the worse part safety to virtue. But the divine judgment approved those who thought virtue was above what is useful, while it condemned those who preferred what seemed more in accordance with safety than with what is virtuous.

Chapter 9.

Cheating and dishonest ways of making money are utterly unfit for clerics whose duty is to serve all. They ought never to be involved in a money affair, unless it is one affecting a man's life. For them the example of David is given, that they should injure none, even when provoked; also the death of Naboth, to keep them from preferring life to virtue.

57. Nothing is more odious than for a man to have no love for a virtuous life, but instead to be kept excited by an unworthy business in following out a low line of trade, or to be inflamed by an avaricious heart, and by day and by night to be eager to damage another's property, not to raise the soul to the splendour of a virtuous life, and not to regard the beauty of true praise.

58. Hence rise inheritances sought by cunning words and gained under pretence of being self-restrained and serious. But this is absolutely abhorrent to the idea of a Christian man. For everything gained by craft and got together by cheating loses the merit of openness. Even among those who have undertaken no duty in the ranks of the clergy it is considered unfitting to seek for the inheritance of another. Let those who are reaching the end of their life use their own judgment, so that they may freely make their wills as they think best, since they will not be able to amend them later. For it is not honourable to divert the savings that belong to others or have been got together for them. It is further the duty of the priest or the cleric to be of use if possible to all and to be harmful to none.

59. If it is not possible to help one without injuring another, it is better to help neither than to press hard upon one. Therefore it is not a priest's duty to interfere in money affairs. For here it must often happen that he who loses his case receives harm; and then he considers that he has been worsted through the action of the intervener. It is a priest's duty to hurt no one, to be ready to help all. To be able to do this is in God's power alone. In a case of life and death, without doubt it is a grave sin to injure him whom one ought to help when in danger. But it is foolish to gain others' hate in taking up money matters, though for the sake of a man's safety great trouble and toil may often be undertaken. It is glorious in such a case to run risks. Let, then, this be firmly held to in the priestly duties, namely, to injure none, not even

Book Three

when provoked and embittered by some injury. Good was the man who said: If I have rewarded evil to those who did me good. For what glory is it if we do not injure him who has not injured us? But it is true virtue to forgive when injured.

60. What a virtuous action was that, when David wished rather to spare the king his enemy, though he could have injured him! How useful, too, it was, for it helped him when he succeeded to the throne. For all learned to observe faith to their king and not to seize the kingdom, but to fear and reverence him. Thus what is virtuous was preferred to what was useful, and then usefulness followed on what was virtuous.

61. But that he spared him was a small matter; he also grieved for him when slain in war, and mourned for him with tears, saying: You mountains of Gilboa, let neither dew nor rain fall upon you; ye mountains of death, for there the shield of the mighty is cast away, the shield of Saul. It is not anointed with oil, but with the blood of the wounded and the fat of the warriors. The bow of Jonathan turned not back and the sword of Saul returned not empty. Saul and Jonathan were lovely and very dear, inseparable in life, and in death they were not divided. They were swifter than eagles, they were stronger than lions. You daughters of Israel, weep over Saul, who clothed you in scarlet with your ornaments, who put on gold upon your apparel. How are the mighty fallen in the midst of the battle! Jonathan was wounded even to death. I am distressed for you, my brother Jonathan; very pleasant have you been unto me. Your love came to me like the love of women. How have the mighty fallen and the longed-for weapons perished!

62. What mother could weep thus for her only son as he wept here for his enemy? Who could follow his benefactor with such praise as that with which he followed the man who plotted against his life? How affectionately he grieved, with what deep feeling he bewailed him! The mountains dried up at the prophet's curse, and a divine power filled the judgment of him who spoke it. Therefore the elements themselves paid the penalty for witnessing the king's death.

63. And what, in the case of holy Naboth, was the cause of his death, except his regard for a virtuous life? For when the king demanded the vineyard from him, promising to give him money, he refused the price for his father's heritage as unseemly, and preferred to shun such shame by dying. The Lord forbid it me, that I should give the inheritance of

my fathers unto you; that is, that such reproach may not fall on me, that God may not allow such wickedness to be attained by force. He is not speaking about the vines— nor has God care for vines or plots of ground— but he says it of his fathers' rights. He could have received another or the king's vineyards and been his friend, wherein men think there is no small usefulness so far as this world is concerned. But because it was base he thought it could not be useful, and so he preferred to endure danger with honour intact, rather than gain what was useful to his own disgrace. I am here again speaking of what is commonly understood as useful, not that in which there is the grace of virtuous life.

64. The king could himself have taken it by force, but that he thought too shameless; then when Naboth was dead he grieved. The Lord also declared that the woman's cruelty should be punished by a fitting penalty, because she was unmindful of virtue and preferred a shameful gain.

65. Every kind of unfair action is shameful. Even in common things, false weights and unjust measures are accursed. And if fraud in the market or in business is punished, can it seem free from reproach if found in the midst of the performance of the duties of virtue? Solomon says: A great and a little weight and various measures are an abomination before the Lord. (Proverbs 20:10) Before that it also says: A false balance is abomination to the Lord, but a just weight is acceptable to Him. (Proverbs 11:1)

Chapter 10.

We are warned not only in civil law, but also in the holy Scriptures, to avoid fraud in every agreement, as is clear from the example of Joshua and the Gibeonites.

66. In everything, therefore, good faith is seemly, justice is pleasing, due measure in equity is delightful. But what shall I say about contracts, and especially about the sale of land, or agreements, or covenants? Are there not rules just for the purpose of shutting out all false deceit, and to make him whose deceit is found out liable to double punishment? Everywhere, then, does regard for what is virtuous take the lead; it shuts out deceit, it expels fraud. Wherefore the prophet David has rightly stated his judgment in general, saying: He has done

Book Three

no evil to his neighbour. Fraud, then, ought to be wanting not only in contracts, in which the defects of those things which are for sale are ordered to be recorded (which contracts, unless the vendor has mentioned the defects, are rendered void by an action for fraud, although he has conveyed them fully to the purchaser), but it ought also to be absent in all else. Candour must be shown, the truth must be made known.

67. The divine Scriptures have plainly stated (not indeed a legal rule of the lawyers but) the ancient judgment of the patriarchs on deceit, in that book of the Old Testament which is ascribed to Joshua the son of Nun. When the report had gone forth among the various peoples that the sea was dried up at the crossing of the Hebrews; that water had flowed from the rock; that food was supplied daily from heaven in quantities large enough for so many thousands of the people; that the walls of Jericho had fallen at the sound of the holy trumpets, being overthrown by the noise of the shouts of the people; also, that the king of Ai was conquered and had been hung on a tree until the evening; then the Gibeonites, fearing his strong hand, came with guile, pretending that they were from a land very far away, and by travelling so long had rent their shoes and worn out their clothing, of which they showed proofs that it was growing old. They said, too, that their reason for undergoing so much labour was their desire to obtain peace and to form friendship with the Hebrews, and began to ask Joshua to form an alliance with them. And he, being as yet ignorant of localities, and not knowing anything of the inhabitants, did not see through their deceit, nor did he enquire of God, but readily believed them.

68. So sacred was one's plighted word held in those days that no one would believe that others could try to deceive. Who could find fault with the saints in this, namely, that they should consider others to have the same feelings as themselves, and suppose no one would lie because truth was their own companion? They know not what deceit is, they gladly believe of others what they themselves are, while they cannot suspect others to be what they themselves are not. Hence Solomon says: An innocent man believes every word. (Proverbs 14:15) We must not blame his readiness to believe, but should rather praise his goodness. To know nothing of anything that may injure another, this is to be innocent. And although he is cheated by another, still he thinks well of all, for he thinks there is good faith in all.

69. Induced, therefore, by such considerations to believe them, he made an agreement, he gave them peace, and formed a union with them. But when he came to their country and the deceit was found out—for though they lived quite close they pretended to be strangers—the people of our fathers began to be angry at having been deceived. Joshua, however, thought the peace they had made could not be broken (for it had been confirmed by an oath), for fear that, in punishing the treachery of others, he should be breaking his own pledge. He made them pay the penalty, however, by forcing them to undertake the lowest kind of work. The judgment was mild indeed, but it was a lasting one, for in their duties there abides the punishment of their ancient cunning, handed down to this day (Joshua 9:27) in their hereditary service.

Chapter 11.

Having adduced examples of certain frauds found in a few passages of the rhetoricians, he shows that these and all others are more fully and plainly condemned in Scripture.

70. I shall say nothing of the snapping of fingers, or the naked dancing of the heir, at entering on an inheritance. These are well-known things. Nor will I speak of the mass of fishes gathered up at a pretended fishing expedition to excite the buyer's desires. For why did he show himself so eager for luxuries and delicacies as to allow a fraud of this character?

71. What need is there for me to speak of that well-known story of the pleasant and quiet retreat at Syracuse and of the cunning of a Sicilian? For he having found a stranger, and knowing that he was anxious to buy an estate, asked him to his grounds for a meal. He accepted, and on the following day he came. There the sight of a great number of fishermen met his eyes, and a banquet laid out in the most splendid profusion. In the sight of the guests, fishers were placed in the garden-grounds, where no net had ever been laid before. Each one in turn presented to the guests what he had taken, the fish were placed upon the table, and caught the glance of those who sat there. The stranger wondered at the large quantity of fish and the number of boats there were. The answer given was, that this was the great water supply, and that great numbers of fish came there because of the sweetness of the water. To be brief, he drew on the stranger to be urgent in getting the

grounds, he willingly allows himself to be induced to sell them, and seemingly with a heavy heart he receives the money.

72. On the next day the purchaser comes to the grounds with his friends, but finds no boat there. On asking whether perhaps the fishermen were observing a festival on that day, he is told that, with the exception of yesterday, they were never wont to fish there; but what power had he to proceed against such a fraud, who had so shamefully grasped at such luxuries? For he who convicts another of a fault ought himself to be free from it. I will not therefore include such trifles as these under the power of ecclesiastical censure, for that altogether condemns every desire for dishonourable gain, and briefly, with few words, forbids every sharp and cunning action.

73. And what shall I say of him who claims to be the heir or legatee, on the proof of a will which, though falsified by others, yet was known to be so by him, and who tries to make a gain through another's crime, though even the laws of the state convict him who knowingly makes use of a false will, as guilty of a wrong action. But the law of justice is plain, namely, that a good man ought not to go aside from the truth, nor to inflict an unjust loss on any one, nor to act at all deceitfully or to take part in any fraud.

74. What is clearer, however, on this point than the case of Ananias? He acted falsely as regards the price he got for his land, for he sold it and laid at the apostles' feet part of the price, pretending it was the whole amount. (Acts 5:2) For this he perished as guilty of fraud. He might have offered nothing and have acted so without committing a fraud. But as deceit entered into his action, he gained no favour for his liberality, but paid the penalty for his artifice.

75. The Lord also in the Gospel rejected those coming to Him with guile, saying: The foxes have holes, (Matthew 8:20) for He bids us live in simplicity and innocency of heart. David also says: You have used deceit as a sharp razor, pointing out by this the treacherous man, just as an implement of this kind is used to help adorn a man, yet often wounds him. If any one makes a show of favour and yet plans deceit after the example of the traitor, so as to give up to death him whom he ought to guard, let him be looked on in the light of that instrument which is wont to wound owing to the vice of a drunken mind and a trembling hand. Thus that man drunk with the wine of wickedness

brought death on the high priest Ahimelech, through a terrible act of treachery, because he had received the prophet with hospitality when the king, roused by the stings of envy, was following him.

Chapter 12.

We may make no promise that is wrong, and if we have made an unjust oath, we may not keep it. It is shown that Herod sinned in this respect. The vow taken by Jephtha is condemned, and so are all others which God does not desire to have paid to Him. Lastly, the daughter of Jephtha is compared with the two Pythagoreans and is placed before them.

76. A man's disposition ought to be undefiled and sound, so that he may utter words without dissimulation and possess his vessel in sanctification; (1 Thessalonians 4:6) that he may not delude his brother with false words nor promise anything dishonourable. If he has made such a promise it is far better for him not to fulfil it, rather than to fulfil what is shameful.

77. Often people bind themselves by a solemn oath, and, though they come to know that they ought not to have made the promise, fulfil it in consideration of their oath. This is what Herod did, as we mentioned before. For he made a shameful promise of reward to a dancer— and cruelly performed it. It was shameful, for a kingdom was promised for a dance; and it was cruel, for the death of a prophet is sacrificed for the sake of an oath. How much better perjury would have been than the keeping of such an oath, if indeed that could be called perjury which a drunkard had sworn to in his wine-cups, or an effeminate profligate had promised while the dance was going on. The prophet's head was brought in on a dish, (Mark 6:28) and this was considered an act of good faith when it really was an act of madness!

78. Never shall I be led to believe that the leader Jephtha made his vow otherwise than without thought, when he promised to offer to God whatever should meet him at the threshold of his house on his return. For he repented of his vow, as afterwards his daughter came to meet him. He rent his clothes and said: Alas, my daughter, you have entangled me, you have become a source of trouble unto me. (Judges 11:35) And though with pious fear and reverence he took upon himself the bitter fulfilment of his cruel task, yet he ordered and left to be observed an annual period of grief and mourning for future times. It

was a hard vow, but far more bitter was its fulfilment, while he who carried it out had the greatest cause to mourn. Thus it became a rule and a law in Israel from year to year, as it says: that the daughters of Israel went to lament the daughter of Jephtha the Gileadite four days in a year. (Judges 11:40) I cannot blame the man for holding it necessary to fulfil his vow, but yet it was a wretched necessity which could only be solved by the death of his child.

79. It is better to make no vow than to vow what God does not wish to be paid to Him to Whom the promise was made. In the case of Isaac we have an example, for the Lord appointed a ram to be offered up instead of him. (Genesis 22:13) Therefore it is not always every promise that is to be fulfilled. Nay, the Lord Himself often alters His determination, as the Scriptures point out. For in the book called Numbers He had declared that He would punish the people with death and destroy them, (Numbers 14:12) but afterwards, when besought by Moses, He was reconciled again to them. And again, He said to Moses and Aaron: Separate yourselves from among this congregation that I may consume them in a moment. (Numbers 16:21) And when they separated from the assembly the earth suddenly clave asunder and opened her mouth and swallowed up Dathan and Abiram.

80. That example of Jephtha's daughter is far more glorious and ancient than that of the two Pythagoreans, which is accounted so notable among the philosophers. One of these, when condemned to death by the tyrant Dionysius, and when the day of his death was fixed, asked for leave to be granted him to go home, so as to provide for his family. But for fear that he might break his faith and not return, he offered a surety for his own death, on condition that if he himself were absent on the appointed day, his surety would be ready to die in his stead. The other did not refuse the conditions of suretyship which were proposed and awaited the day of death with a calm mind. So the one did not withdraw himself and the other returned on the day appointed. This all seemed so wonderful that the tyrant sought their friendship whose destruction he had been anxious for.

81. What, then, in the case of esteemed and learned men is full of marvel, that in the case of a virgin is found to be far more splendid, far more glorious, as she says to her sorrowing father: Do to me according to that which has proceeded out of your mouth. (Judges 11:36) But she asked for a delay of two months in order that she might go about with

her companions upon the mountains to bewail fitly and dutifully her virginity now given up to death. The weeping of her companions did not move her, their grief prevailed not upon her, nor did their lamentations hold her back. She allowed not the day to pass, nor did the hour escape her notice. She returned to her father as though returning according to her own desire, and of her own will urged him on when he was hesitating, and acted thus of her own free choice, so that what was at first an awful chance became a pious sacrifice.

Chapter 13.

Judith, after enduring many dangers for virtue's sake, gained very many and great benefits.

82. See! Judith presents herself to you as worthy of admiration. She approaches Holophernes, a man feared by the people, and surrounded by the victorious troops of the Assyrians. At first she makes an impression on him by the grace of her form and the beauty of her countenance. Then she entraps him by the refinement of her speech. Her first triumph was that she returned from the tent of the enemy with her purity unspotted. (Judith 12:20) Her second, that she gained a victory over a man, and put to flight the people by her counsel.

83. The Persians were terrified at her daring. And so what is admired in the case of those two Pythagoreans deserves also in her case our admiration, for she trembled not at the danger of death, nor even at the danger her modesty was in, which is a matter of greater concern to good women. She feared not the blow of one scoundrel, nor even the weapons of a whole army. She, a woman, stood between the lines of the combatants— right amidst victorious arms— heedless of death. As one looks at her overwhelming danger, one would say she went out to die; as one looks at her faith, one says she went but out to fight.

84. Judith then followed the call of virtue, and as she follows that, she wins great benefits. It was virtuous to prevent the people of the Lord from giving themselves up to the heathen; to prevent them from betraying their native rites and mysteries, or from yielding up their consecrated virgins, their venerable widows, and modest matrons to barbarian impurity, or from ending the siege by a surrender. It was virtuous for her to be willing to encounter danger on behalf of all, so as to deliver all from danger.

85. How great must have been the power of her virtue, that she, a woman, should claim to give counsel on the chiefest matters and not leave it in the hands of the leaders of the people! How great, again, the power of her virtue to reckon for certain upon God to help her! How great her grace to find His help!

Chapter 14.

How virtuous and useful was that which Elisha did. This is compared with that oft-recounted act of the Greeks. John gave up his life for virtue's sake, and Susanna for the same reason exposed herself to the danger of death.

86. What did Elisha follow but virtue, when he brought the army of Syria who had come to take him as captive into Samaria, after having covered their eyes with blindness? Then he said: O Lord, open their eyes that they may see. And they saw. But when the king of Israel wished to slay those that had entered and asked the prophet to give him leave to do so, he answered that they whose captivity was not brought about by strength of hand or weapons of war must not be slain, but that rather he should help them by supplying food. Then they were refreshed with plenty of food. And after that those Syrian robbers thought they must never again return to the land of Israel.

87. How much nobler was this than that which the Greeks once did! For when two nations strove one with the other to gain glory and supreme power, and one of them had the opportunity to burn the ships of the other secretly, they thought it a shameful thing to do so, and preferred to gain a less advantage honourably than a greater one in shameful wise. They, indeed, could not act thus without disgrace to themselves, and entrap by this plot those who had banded together for the sake of ending the Persian war. Though they could deny it in word, yet they could never but blush at the thought of it. Elisha, however, wished to save, not destroy, those who were deceived indeed, though not by some foul act, and had been struck blind by the power of the Lord. For it was seemly to spare an enemy, and to grant his life to an adversary when indeed he could have taken it, had he not spared it.

88. It is plain, then, that whatever is seemly is always useful. For holy Judith by seemly disregard for her own safety put an end to the dangers of the siege, and by her own virtue won what was useful to all in

common. And Elisha gained more renown by pardoning than he would have done by slaying, and preserved those enemies whom he had taken for greater usefulness.

89. And what else did John have in mind but what is virtuous, so that he could not endure a wicked union even in the king's case, saying: It is not lawful for you to have her to wife. (Matthew 14:4) He could have been silent, had he not thought it unseemly for himself not to speak the truth for fear of death, or to make the prophetic office yield to the king, or to indulge in flattery. He knew well that he would die as he was against the king, but he preferred virtue to safety. Yet what is more expedient than the suffering which brought glory to the saint.

90. Holy Susanna, too, when threatened with the fear of false witness, seeing herself hard pressed on one side by danger, on the other by disgrace, preferred to avoid disgrace by a virtuous death rather than to endure and live a shameful life in the desire to save herself. So while she fixed her mind on virtue, she also preserved her life. But if she had preferred what seemed to her to be useful to preserve life, she would never have gained such great renown, nay, perhaps— and that would have been not only useless but even dangerous— she might even not have escaped the penalty for her crime. We note, therefore, that whatsoever is shameful cannot be useful, nor, again, can that which is virtuous be useless. For usefulness is ever the double of virtue, and virtue of usefulness.

Chapter 15.

After mentioning a noble action of the Romans, the writer shows from the deeds of Moses that he had the greatest regard for what is virtuous.

91. It is related as a memorable deed of a Roman general, that when the physician of a hostile king came to him and promised to give him poison, he sent him back bound to the enemy. In truth, it is a noble thing for a man to refuse to gain the victory by foul acts, after he has entered on the struggle for power. He did not consider virtue to lie in victory, but declared that to be a shameful victory unless it was gained with honour.

92. Let us return to our hero Moses, and to loftier deeds, to show they were both superior as well as earlier. The king of Egypt would not let the people of our fathers go. Then Moses bade the priest Aaron to stretch his rod over all the waters of Egypt. Aaron stretched it out, and the water of the river was turned into blood. (Exodus 7:19) None could drink the water, and all the Egyptians were perishing with thirst; but there was pure water flowing in abundance for the fathers. They sprinkled ashes toward heaven, and sores and burning boils came upon man and beast. (Exodus 9:10) They brought down hail mingled with flaming fire, and all things were destroyed upon the land. (Exodus 9:23) Moses prayed, and all things were restored to their former beauty. The hail ceased, the sores were healed, the rivers gave their wonted draught. (Exodus 9:29)

93. Then, again, the land was covered with thick darkness for the space of three days, because Moses had raised his hand and spread out the darkness. (Exodus 10:22) All the first-born of Egypt died, while all the offspring of the Hebrews was left unharmed. (Exodus 12:29) Moses was asked to put an end to these horrors, and he prayed and obtained his request. In the one case it was a fact worthy of praise that he checked himself from joining in deceit; in the other it was noteworthy how, by his innate goodness, he turned aside from the foe those divinely ordered punishments. He was indeed, as it is written, gentle and meek. (Numbers 12:3) He knew that the king would not keep true to his promises, yet he thought it right and good to pray when asked to do so, to bless when wronged, to forgive when besought.

94. He cast down his rod and it became a serpent which devoured the serpents of Egypt; (Exodus 7:12) this signifying that the Word should become Flesh to destroy the poison of the dread serpent by the forgiveness and pardon of sins. For the rod stands for the Word that is true— royal— filled with power— and glorious in ruling. The rod became a serpent; so He Who was the Son of God begotten of the Father became the Son of man born of a woman, and lifted, like the serpent, on the cross, poured His healing medicine on the wounds of man. Wherefore the Lord Himself says: As Moses lifted up the serpent in the wilderness, so must the Son of Man be lifted up. (John 3:14)

95. Again, another sign which Moses gave points to our Lord Jesus Christ. He put his hand into his bosom, and drew it out again, and his hand was become as snow. A second time he put it in and drew it out,

and it was again like the appearance of human flesh. (Exodus 4:6-7) This signified first the original glory of the Godhead of the Lord Jesus, and then the assumption of our flesh, in which truth all nations and peoples must believe. So he put in his hand, for Christ is the right hand of God; and whosoever does not believe in His Godhead and Incarnation is punished as a sinner; like that king who, while not believing open and plain signs, yet afterwards, when punished, prayed that he might find mercy. How great, then, Moses' regard for virtue must have been is shown by these proofs, and especially by the fact that he offered himself on behalf of the people, praying that God would either forgive the people or blot him out of the book of the living. (Exodus 32:32)

Chapter 16.

After saying a few words about Tobit he demonstrates that Raguel surpassed the philosophers in virtue.

96. Tobit also clearly portrayed in his life true virtue, when he left the feast and buried the dead, (Tobit 2:4) and invited the needy to the meals at his own poor table. And Raguel is a still brighter example. For he, in his regard for virtue, when asked to give his daughter in marriage, was not silent regarding his daughter's faults, for fear of seeming to get the better of the suitor by silence. So when Tobit the son of Tobias asked that his daughter might be given him, he answered that, according to the law, she ought to be given him as near of kin, but that he had already given her to six men, and all of them were dead. (Tobit 7:11) This just man, then, feared more for others than for himself, and wished rather that his daughter should remain unmarried than that others should run risks in consequence of their union with her.

97. How simply he settled all the questions of the philosophers! They talk about the defects of a house, whether they ought to be concealed or made known by the vendor. Raguel was quite certain that his daughter's faults ought not to be kept secret. And, indeed, he had not been eager to give her up— he was asked for her. We can have no doubt how much more nobly he acted than those philosophers, when we consider how much more important a daughter's future is than some mere money affair.

Book Three

Chapter 17.

With what virtuous feelings the fathers of old hid the sacred fires when on the point of going into captivity.

98. Let us consider, again, that deed done at the time of the captivity, which has attained the highest degree of virtue and glory. Virtue is checked by no adversities, for it rises up among them, and prevails here rather than in prosperity. 'Mid chains or arms, 'mid flames or slavery (which is harder for freemen to bear than any punishment), 'midst the pains of the dying, the destruction of their country, the fears of the living, or the blood of the slain,— amidst all this our forefathers failed not in their care and thought for what is virtuous. Amidst the ashes and dust of their fallen country it glowed and shone forth brightly in pious efforts.

99. For when our fathers were carried away into Persia, (2 Maccabees 1:19) certain priests, who then were in the service of Almighty God, secretly buried in the valley the fire taken from the altar of the Lord. There was there an open pit, with no water in it, and not accessible for the wants of the people, in a spot unknown and free from intruders. There they sealed the hidden fire with the sacred mark and in secret. They were not anxious to bury gold or to hide up silver to preserve it for their children, but in their own great peril, thinking of all that was virtuous, they thought the sacred fire ought to be preserved so that impure men might not defile it, nor the blood of the slain extinguish it, nor the heaps of miserable ruins cover it.

100. So they went to Persia, free only in their religion; for that alone could not be torn from them by their captivity. After a length of time, indeed, according to God's good pleasure, He put it into the Persian king's heart to order the temple in Judea to be restored, and the regular customs to be again rebuilt at Jerusalem. To carry out this work of his the Persian king appointed the priest Nehemiah. He took with him the grandchildren of those priests who on leaving their native soil had hidden the sacred fire to save it from perishing. But on arriving, as we are told in the history of the fathers, they found not fire but water. And when fire was wanting to burn upon the altars, the priest Nehemiah bade them draw the water, to bring it to him, and to sprinkle it upon the wood. Then, O wondrous sight! Though the sky had been overcast with clouds, suddenly the sun shone forth, a great fire flamed forth, so

that all, wonder-stricken at such a clear sign of the favour of the Lord, were filled with joy. Nehemiah prayed; the priests sang a hymn of praise to God, when the sacrifice was completed. Nehemiah again bade the remainder of the water to be poured upon the larger stones. And when this was done a flame burst forth while the light shining from off the altar shone more brightly yet.

101. When this sign became known, the king of Persia ordered a temple to be built on that spot where the fire had been hidden and the water afterwards found, to which many gifts were made. They who were with holy Nehemiah called it Naphthar, (2 Maccabbees 1:36) — which means cleansing— by many it is called Nephi. It is to be found also in the history of the prophet Jeremiah, that he bade those who should come after him to take of the fire. That is the fire which fell on Moses' sacrifice and consumed it, as it is written: There came a fire out from the Lord and consumed upon the altar all the whole burnt-offering. (Leviticus 9:24) The sacrifice must be hallowed with this fire only. Therefore, also, fire went out from the Lord upon the sons of Aaron who wished to offer strange fire, and consumed them, so that their dead bodies were cast forth without the camp. (Leviticus 10:2)

101. Jeremiah coming to a spot found there a house like a cave, and brought into it the tabernacle, the ark, and the altar of incense, and closed up the entrance. And when those who had come with him examined it rather closely to mark the spot, they could not discover nor find it. When Jeremiah understood what they wanted he said: The spot will remain unknown until God shall gather His people together and be gracious to them. Then God shall reveal these things and the majesty of the Lord shall appear. (2 Maccabbees 2:5)

Chapter 18.

In the narration of that event already mentioned, and especially of the sacrifice offered by Nehemiah, is typified the Holy Spirit and Christian baptism. The sacrifice of Moses and Elijah and the history of Noah are also referred to the same.

102. We form the congregation of the Lord. We recognize the propitiation of our Lord God, which our Propitiator wrought in His passion. I think, too, we cannot leave out of sight that fire when we read that the Lord Jesus baptizes with the Holy Spirit and with fire, (John 1:33) as John

said in his Gospel. Rightly was the sacrifice consumed, for it was for sin. But that fire was a type of the Holy Spirit Who was to come down after the Lord's ascension, and forgive the sins of all, and Who like fire inflames the mind and faithful heart. Wherefore Jeremiah, after receiving the Spirit, says: It became in my heart as a burning fire flaming in my bones, and I am vile and cannot bear it. (Jeremiah 20:9) In the Acts of the Apostles, also, when the Holy Spirit descended upon the apostles and those others who were waiting for the Promise of the Father, we read that tongues as of fire were distributed among them. (Acts 2:3) The soul of each one was so uplifted by His influence that they were supposed to be full of new wine, (Acts 2:13) who instead had received the gift of a diversity of tongues.

103. What else can this mean— namely, that fire became water and water called forth fire— but that spiritual grace burns out our sins through fire, and through water cleanses them? For sin is washed away and it is burnt away. Wherefore the Apostle says: The fire shall try every man's work of what sort it is. (1 Corinthians 3:13) And further on: If any man's work shall be burned, he shall suffer loss: but he himself shall be saved; yet so as by fire. (1 Corinthians 3:15)

104. This, then, we have stated, so as to prove that sins are burnt out by means of fire. We know now that this is in truth the sacred fire which then, as a type of the future remission of sins, came down upon the sacrifice.

105. This fire is hidden in the time of captivity, during which sin reigns, but in the time of liberty it is brought forth. And though it is changed into the appearance of water, yet it preserves its nature as fire so as to consume the sacrifice. Do not wonder when you read that God the Father said: I am a consuming fire. (Deuteronomy 4:24) And again: They have forsaken Me, the fountain of living water. (Jeremiah 2:13) The Lord Jesus, too, like a fire inflamed the hearts of those who heard Him, and like a fount of waters cooled them. For He Himself said in His Gospel that He came to send fire on the earth (Luke 12:49) and to supply a draught of living waters to those who thirst. (John 7:37-38)

106. In the time of Elijah, also, fire came down when he challenged the prophets of the heathen to light up the altar without fire. When they could not do so, he poured water thrice over his victim, so that the

water ran round about the altar; then he cried out and the fire fell from the Lord from heaven and consumed the burnt-offering.

107. You are that victim. Contemplate in silence each single point. The breath of the Holy Spirit descends on you, He seems to burn you when He consumes your sins. The sacrifice which was consumed in the time of Moses was a sacrifice for sin, wherefore Moses said, as is written in the book of the Maccabees: Because the sacrifice for sin was not to be eaten, it was consumed. (2 Maccabees 2:11) Does it not seem to be consumed for you when in the sacrament of baptism the whole outer man perishes? Our old man is crucified, (Romans 6:6) the Apostle exclaims. Herein, as the example of the fathers teaches us, the Egyptian is swallowed up— the Hebrew arises renewed by the Holy Spirit, as he also crossed the Red Sea dryshod— where our fathers were baptized in the cloud and in the sea. (1 Corinthians 10:1-2)

108. In the flood, too, in Noah's time all flesh died, though just Noah was preserved together with his family. (Genesis 7:23) Is not a man consumed when all that is mortal is cut off from life? The outer man is destroyed, but the inner is renewed. Not in baptism alone but also in repentance does this destruction of the flesh tend to the growth of the spirit, as we are taught on the Apostle's authority, when holy Paul says: I have judged as though I were present him that has so done this deed, to deliver him unto Satan for the destruction of the flesh, that the spirit may be saved in the day of our Lord Jesus Christ.

109. We seem to have made a somewhat lengthy digression for the sake of regarding this wonderful mystery, in desiring to unfold more fully this sacrament which has been revealed to us, and which, indeed, is as full of virtue as it is full of religious awe.

Chapter 19.

The crime committed by the inhabitants of Gibeah against the wife of a certain Levite is related, and from the vengeance taken it is inferred how the idea of virtue must have filled the heart of those people of old.

110. What regard for virtue our forefathers had to avenge by a war the wrongs of one woman which had been brought on her by her violation at the hands of profligate men! Nay, when the people were conquered, they vowed that they would not give their daughters in marriage to the

Book Three

tribe of Benjamin! That tribe had remained without hope of posterity, had they not received leave of necessity to use deceit. And this permission does not seem to fail in giving fitting punishment for violation, since they were only allowed to enter on a union by a rape, and not through the sacrament of marriage. And indeed it was right that they who had broken another's intercourse should themselves lose their marriage rites.

111. How full of pitiful traits is this story! A man, it says, (Judges 19:1-3) a Levite, had taken to himself a wife, who I suppose was called a concubine from the word concubitus. She some time afterwards, as is wont to happen, offended at certain things, betook herself to her father, and was with him four months. Then her husband arose and went to the house of his father-in-law, to reconcile himself with his wife, to win her back and take her home again. The woman ran to meet him and brought her husband into her father's house.

112. The maiden's Judges 4-9 father rejoiced and went to meet him, and the man stayed with him three days, and they ate and rested. On the next day the Levite arose at daybreak, but was detained by his father-in-law, that he might not so quickly lose the pleasure of his company. Again on the next and the third day the maiden's father did not suffer his son-in-law to start, until their joy and mutual regard was complete. But on the seventh day, when it was already drawing to a close, after a pleasant meal, having urged the approach of the coming night, so as to make him think he ought to sleep among friends rather than strangers, he was unable to keep him, and so let him go together with his daughter.

113. When some little progress (Judges 19:10-21) was made, though night was threatening to come on, and they were close by the town of the Jebusites, on the slave's request that his lord should turn aside there, he refused, because it was not a city of the children of Israel. He meant to get as far as Gibeah, which was inhabited by the people of the tribe of Benjamin. But when they arrived there was no one to receive them with hospitality, except a stranger of advanced age— When he had looked upon them he asked the Levite: Where are you going, and where are you coming from? On his answering that he was travelling and was making for Mount Ephraim and that there was no one to take him in, the old man offered him hospitality and prepared a meal.

114. And when they were satisfied (Judges 19:22-26) and the tables were removed, vile men rushed up and surrounded the house. Then the old man offered these wicked men his daughter, a virgin, and the concubine with whom she shared her bed, only that violence might not be inflicted on his guest. But when reason did no good and violence prevailed, the Levite parted from his wife, and they knew her and abused her all that night. Overcome by this cruelty or by grief at her wrong, she fell at the door of their host where her husband had entered, and gave up the ghost, with the last effort of her life guarding the feelings of a good wife so as to preserve for her husband at least her mortal remains.

115. When this became known (to be brief) almost all the people of Israel broke out into war. The war remained doubtful with an uncertain issue, but in the third engagement the people of Benjamin were delivered to the people of Israel, (Judges 20:48) and being condemned by the divine judgment paid the penalty for their profligacy. The sentence, further, was that none of the people of the fathers should give his daughter in marriage to them. This was confirmed by a solemn oath. But relenting at having laid so hard a sentence on their brethren, they moderated their severity so as to give them in marriage those maidens that had lost their parents, whose fathers had been slain for their sins, or to give them the means of finding a wife by a raid. Because of the villainy of so foul a deed, they who have violated another's marriage rights were shown to be unworthy to ask for marriage. But for fear that one tribe might perish from the people, they connived at the deceit.

116. What great regard our forefathers had for virtue is shown by the fact that forty thousand men drew the sword against their brethren of the tribe of Benjamin in their desire to avenge the wrong done to modesty, for they would not endure the violation of chastity. And so in that war on both sides there fell sixty-five thousand warriors, while their cities were burnt. And when at first the people of Israel were defeated, yet unmoved by fear at the reverses of the war, they disregarded the sorrow the avenging of chastity cost them. They rushed into the battle ready to wash out with their own blood the stains of the crime that had been committed.

Book Three

Chapter 20.

After the terrible siege of Samaria was ended in accordance with Elisha's prophecy, he relates what regard the four lepers showed for what was virtuous.

117. Why need we wonder that the people of the Lord had regard for what was seemly and virtuous when even the lepers— as we read in the books of the Kings— showed concern for what is virtuous?

118. There was a great famine in Samaria, for the army of the Syrians was besieging it. The king in his anxiety was making the round of the guards on the walls when a woman addressed him, saying: This woman persuaded me to give up my son— and I gave him up, and we boiled him and ate him. And she promised that she would afterwards bring her son and that we should eat his flesh together, but now she has hidden her son and will not bring him. The king was troubled because these women seemed to have fed not merely on human bodies, but on the bodies of their own children; and being moved by an example of such awful misery, threatened the prophet Elisha with death. For he believed it was in his power to break up the siege and to avert the famine; or else he was angry because the prophet had not allowed the king to smite the Syrians whom he had struck with blindness.

119. Elisha sat with the elders at Bethel, and before the king's messenger came to him he said to the elders: See ye how the son of that murderess has sent to take away mine head? Then the messenger entered and brought the king's command threatening instant danger to his life. Him the prophet answered: Tomorrow about this time shall a measure of fine flour be sold for a shekel, and two measures of barley for a shekel in the gate of Samaria. Then when the messenger sent by the king would not believe it, saying: If the Lord would rain abundance of grain from heaven, not even so would that come about, Elisha said to him: Because you have not believed, you shall see it with your eyes, but shall not eat of it.

120. And suddenly in the camp of Syria was there heard, as it were, a sound of chariots and a loud noise of horses and the noise of a great host, and the tumult of some vast battle. And the Syrians thought that the king of Israel had called to his help in the battle the king of Egypt and the king of the Amorites, and they fled at dawn leaving their tents,

for they feared that they might be crushed by the sudden arrival of fresh foes, and would not be able to withstand the united forces of the kings. This was unknown in Samaria, for they dared not go out of the town, being overcome with fear and also being weak through hunger.

121. But there were four lepers at the gate of the city to whom life was a misery, and to die would be gain. And they said one to another: Behold we sit here and die. If we enter into the city, we shall die with hunger; if we remain here, there are no means of living at hand for us. Let us go to the Syrian camp, either they will quickly kill us or grant us the means of safety. So they went and entered into the camp, and behold, all was forsaken by the enemy. Entering the tents, first of all on finding food they satisfied their hunger, then they laid hold of as much gold and silver as they could. But while they were intent on the booty alone, they arranged to announce to the king that the Syrians had fled, for they thought this more virtuous than to withhold the information and keep for themselves the plunder gained by deceit.

122. At this information the people went forth and plundered the Syrian camp. The supplies of the enemy produced an abundance, and brought about cheapness of grain according to the prophet's word: A measure of fine flour for a shekel, and two measures of barley for a shekel. In this rejoicing of the people, that officer on whose hand the king leaned died, being crushed and trodden under foot by the people as the crowds kept hurrying to go out or returned with great rejoicing.

Chapter 21.

Esther in danger of her life followed the grace of virtue; nay, even a heathen king did so, when death was threatened to a man most friendly to him. For friendship must ever be combined with virtue, as the examples of Jonathan and Ahimelech show.

123. Why did Queen Esther (Esther 4:16) expose herself to death and not fear the wrath of a fierce king? Was it not to save her people from death, an act both seemly and virtuous? The king of Persia himself also, though fierce and proud, yet thought it seemly to show honour to the man who had given information about a plot which had been laid against himself, (Esther 6:10) to save a free people from slavery, to snatch them from death, and not to spare him who had pressed on such unseemly plans. So finally he handed over to the gallows (Esther 7:9-10) the

man that stood second to himself, and whom he counted chief among all his friends, because he considered that he had dishonoured him by his false counsels.

124. For that commendable friendship which maintains virtue is to be preferred most certainly to wealth, or honours, or power. It is not wont to be preferred to virtue indeed, but to follow after it. So it was with Jonathan, who for his affection's sake avoided not his father's displeasure nor the danger to his own safety. So, too, it was with Ahimelech, who, to preserve the duties of hospitality, thought he must endure death rather than betray his friend when fleeing.

Chapter 22.

Virtue must never be given up for the sake of a friend. If, however, one has to bear witness against a friend, it must be done with caution. Between friends what candour is needed in opening the heart, what magnanimity in suffering, what freedom in finding fault! Friendship is the guardian of virtues, which are not to be found but in men of like character. It must be mild in rebuking and averse to seeking its own advantage; whence it happens that true friends are scarce among the rich. What is the dignity of friendship? The treachery of a friend, as it is worse, so it is also more hateful than another's, as is recognized from the example of Judas and of Job's friends.

125. Nothing, then, must be set before virtue; and that it may never be set aside by the desire for friendship, Scripture also gives us a warning on the subject of friendship. There are, indeed various questions raised among philosophers; for instance whether a man ought for the sake of a friend to plot against his country or not, so as to serve his friend? Whether it is right to break one's faith, and so aid and maintain a friend's advantage?

126. And Scripture also says: A maul, and a sword, and a sharp arrow, so is a man that bears false witness against his friend. (Proverbs 25:18) But note what it adds. It blames not witness given against a friend, but false witness. For what if the cause of God or of one's country compels one to give witness? Ought friendship to take a higher place than our religion, or our love for our fellow citizens? In these matters, however, true witness is required so that a friend may not be assailed by the treachery of a friend, by whose good faith he ought to be acquitted. A

man, then, ought never to please a friend who desires evil, or to plot against one who is innocent.

127. Certainly, if it is necessary to give witness, then, when one knows of any fault in a friend, one ought to rebuke him secretly— if he does not listen, one must do it openly. For rebukes are good, and often better than a silent friendship. Even if a friend thinks himself hurt, still rebuke him; and if the bitterness of the correction wounds his mind, still rebuke him and fear not. The wounds of a friend are better than the kisses of flatterers. (Proverbs 27:6) Rebuke, then, your erring friend; forsake not an innocent one. For friendship ought to be steadfast and to rest firm in true affection. We ought not to change our friends in childish fashion at some idle fancy.

128. Open your breast to a friend that he may be faithful to you, and that you may receive from him the delight of your life. For a faithful friend is the medicine of life and the grace of immortality. (Sirach 6:16) Give way to a friend as to an equal, and be not ashamed to be beforehand with your friend in doing kindly duties. For friendship knows nothing of pride. So the wise man says: Do not blush to greet a friend. (Sirach 22:25) Do not desert a friend in time of need, nor forsake him nor fail him, for friendship is the support of life. Let us then bear our burdens as the Apostle has taught: (Galatians 6:2) for he spoke to those whom the charity of the same one body had embraced together. If friends in prosperity help friends, why do they not also in times of adversity offer their support? Let us aid by giving counsel, let us offer our best endeavours, let us sympathize with them with all our heart.

129. If necessary, let us endure for a friend even hardship. Often enmity has to be borne for the sake of a friend's innocence; oftentimes revilings, if one defends and answers for a friend who is found fault with and accused. Do not be afraid of such displeasure, for the voice of the just says: Though evil come upon me, I will endure it for a friend's sake. (Sirach 22:26) In adversity, too, a friend is proved, for in prosperity all seem to be friends. But as in adversity patience and endurance are needed, so in prosperity strong influence is wanted to check and confute the arrogance of a friend who becomes overbearing.

130. How nobly Job when he was in adversity said: Pity me, my friends, pity me. (Job 19:21) That is not a cry as it were of misery, but rather one of blame. For when he was unjustly reproached by his

friends, he answered: Pity me, my friends, that is, you ought to show pity, but instead ye assail and overwhelm a man with whose sufferings ye ought to show sympathy for friendship's sake.

131. Preserve, then, my sons, that friendship you have begun with your brethren, for nothing in the world is more beautiful than that. It is indeed a comfort in this life to have one to whom you can open your heart, with whom you can share confidences, and to whom you can entrust the secrets of your heart. It is a comfort to have a trusty man by your side, who will rejoice with you in prosperity, sympathize in troubles, encourage in persecution. What good friends those Hebrew children were whom the flames of the fiery furnace did not separate from their love of each other! Of them we have already spoken. Holy David says well: Saul and Jonathan were lovely and pleasant, inseparable in their life, in death they were not divided.

132. This is the fruit of friendship; and so faith may not be put aside for the sake of friendship. He cannot be a friend to a man who has been unfaithful to God. Friendship is the guardian of pity and the teacher of equality, so as to make the superior equal to the inferior, and the inferior to the superior. For there can be no friendship between diverse characters, and so the good-will of either ought to be mutually suited to the other. Let not authority be wanting to the inferior if the matter demands it, nor humility to the superior. Let him listen to the other as though he were of like position— an equal, and let the other warn and reprove like a friend, not from a desire to show off, but with a deep feeling of love.

134. Let not your warning be harsh, nor your rebuke bitter, for as friendship ought to avoid flattery, so, too, ought it to be free from arrogance. For what is a friend but a partner in love, to whom you unite and attachest your soul, and with whom you blend so as to desire from being two to become one; to whom you entrust yourself as to a second self, from whom you fear nothing, and from whom you demand nothing dishonourable for the sake of your own advantage. Friendship is not meant as a source of revenue, but is full of seemliness, full of grace. Friendship is a virtue, not a way of making money. It is produced, not by money, but by esteem; not by the offer of rewards, but by a mutual rivalry in doing kindnesses.

134. Lastly, the friendships of the poor are generally better than those of the rich, and often the rich are without friends, while the poor have many. For true friendship cannot exist where there is lying flattery. Many try fawningly to please the rich, but no one cares to make pretence to a poor man. Whatsoever is stated to a poor man is true, his friendship is free from envy.

135. What is more precious than friendship which is shared alike by angels and by men? Wherefore the Lord Jesus says: Make to yourselves friends of the mammon of unrighteousness, that they may receive you into eternal habitations. (Luke 16:9) God Himself makes us friends instead of servants, as He Himself says: You are My friends if you do whatsoever I command you. (John 15:14) He gave us a pattern of friendship to follow. We are to fulfil the wish of a friend, to unfold to him our secrets which we hold in our own hearts, and are not to disregard his confidences. Let us show him our heart and he will open his to us. Therefore He says: I have called you friends, for I have made known unto you all things whatsoever I have heard of My Father. (John 15:15) A friend, then, if he is a true one, hides nothing; he pours forth his soul as the Lord Jesus poured forth the mysteries of His Father.

136. So he who does the will of God is His friend and is honoured with this name. He who is of one mind with Him, he too is His friend. For there is unity of mind in friends, and no one is more hateful than the man that injures friendship. Hence in the traitor the Lord found this the worst point on which to condemn his treachery, namely, that he gave no sign of gratitude and had mingled the poison of malice at the table of friendship. So He says: It was thou, a man of like mind, My guide and Mine acquaintance, who ever took pleasant meals with Me. That is: it could not be endured, for you fell upon Him Who granted grace to you. For if My enemy had reproached Me I could have borne it, and I would have hid Myself from him who hated Me. An enemy can be avoided; a friend cannot, if he desires to lay a plot. Let us guard against him to whom we do not entrust our plans; we cannot guard against him to whom we have already entrusted them. And so to show up all the hatefulness of the sin He did not say: Thou, My servant, My apostle; but thou, a man of like mind with Me; that is: you are not My but your own betrayer, for you betrayed a man of like mind with yourself.

137. The Lord Himself, when He was displeased with the three princes who had not deferred to holy Job, wished to pardon them through their friend, so that the prayer of friendship might win remission of sins. Therefore Job asked and God pardoned. Friendship helped them whom arrogance had harmed. (Job 42:7-8)

138. These things I have left with you, my children, that you may guard them in your minds— you yourselves will prove whether they will be of any advantage. Meanwhile they offer you a large number of examples, for almost all the examples drawn from our forefathers, and also many a word of theirs, are included within these three books; so that, although the language may not be graceful, yet a succession of old-time examples set down in such small compass may offer much instruction.

Also from Benediction Books ...
Wandering Between Two Worlds: Essays on Faith and Art
Anita Mathias
Benediction Books, 2007
152 pages
ISBN: 0955373700

Available from www.amazon.com, www.amazon.co.uk

In these wide-ranging lyrical essays, Anita Mathias writes, in lush, lovely prose, of her naughty Catholic childhood in Jamshedpur, India; her large, eccentric family in Mangalore, a sea-coast town converted by the Portuguese in the sixteenth century; her rebellion and atheism as a teenager in her Himalayan boarding school, run by German missionary nuns, St. Mary's Convent, Nainital; and her abrupt religious conversion after which she entered Mother Teresa's convent in Calcutta as a novice. Later rich, elegant essays explore the dualities of her life as a writer, mother, and Christian in the United States-- Domesticity and Art, Writing and Prayer, and the experience of being "an alien and stranger" as an immigrant in America, sensing the need for roots.

About the Author

Anita Mathias was born in India, has a B.A. and M.A. in English from Somerville College, Oxford University and an M.A. in Creative Writing from the Ohio State University. Her essays have been published in The Washington Post, The London Magazine, The Virginia Quarterly Review, Commonweal, Notre Dame Magazine, America, The Christian Century, Religion Online, The Southwest Review, Contemporary Literary Criticism, New Letters, The Journal, and two of HarperSanFrancisco's The Best Spiritual Writing anthologies. Her non-fiction has won fellowships from The National Endowment for the Arts; The Minnesota State Arts Board; The Jerome Foundation, The Vermont Studio Center; The Virginia Centre for the Creative Arts, and the First Prize for the Best General Interest Article from the Catholic Press Association of the United States and Canada. Anita has taught Creative Writing at the College of William and Mary, and now lives and writes in Oxford, England.

www.anitamathias.com
wanderingbetweentwoworlds.blogspot.com (General and Culture)
thegoodbooksblog.blogspot.com (Reading and Writing)
theoxfordchristian.blogspot.com (Christian)

CPSIA information can be obtained
at www.ICGtesting.com
Printed in the USA
BVHW08s1457030918
526339BV00002B/51/P